Crime
Scenes

GINA GALLO

ISBN: 0-9678809-1-2

For Insane Fish everywhere.

These stories are based on the true experiences of Chicago Police officers and the citizens they serve. To protect their privacy, all names, locations and personal identifiers have been changed.

Roll Call

The following sworn and civilian personnel are acknowledged with love and thanks. You fed my dreams, watched my back and kept me alive to tell the tales.

Chicago Police Department Sworn Personnel

Officer 'Bongo Ron' Paliga - czar of Zone 6, who had the vision, kept the faith, and made me believe in life after blue.

Officer Daisy the Druid - sister, seer, and soul survivor - in this life and all the others.

Officer P. 'Mr. Pliers' Hernandez - my Lincoln unit from the Academy to the smoking gun.

Officer Brandon Medow- your assist was murder, and the chili's still pending.

Lieutenant Dennis Banahan - my 69th Street paisan and co-conspirator.

Auxiliary Law Enforcement Personnel

Special thanks and love to my paisans, friends, and long-distance back-up who never fail to answer my 10-1.

Sgt. Thomas R. Westfall - Community Police and Training.

Marshall County, West Virginia Sheriff's Dept.

Chief Kenneth H. Robison, Sr. - Director, State of South Carolina Security Enforcement Agency.

Gary McNabb, Armorer - Greensboro Police Dept., Greensboro, NC.

Officer Joseph Mormello - Philadelphia. Police Dept., Philadelphia, PA.

Sgt. John Kreuger - Georgia Public Service Commission.

Inv. Rob Hall - Essex County Sheriff's Office, Essex County, VA.

Civilian Personnel

Hugs and thanks to these special friends:

Milo Gun - for green lions and blue dreams against all odds.

Dave and Dodge - for gifts of faith, acts of love, works of genius.

Stephanie - the hands-down (face down) coolest body of evidence

Ron Dionne - for lending your New York brain to this Chicago heart.

Eric and Brett - the men of Company G.

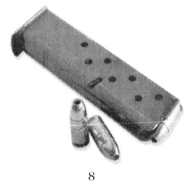

"Gina Gallo takes us on a scintillating walk along Chicago's dark streets. Don't expect the usual bullshit Hollywood version of police officers. Gallo's cops are as real as fresh blood on a tenement floor, as chilling as out-gunned undercover cops caught in a deadly shootout, as sexy as a woman who could jump-start a dead man.

If you want to know how cops feel, what they think, what they REALLY go through on a daily (and nightly) basis, buy this book."

O'Neil De Noux
Homicide Detective-turned-writer
Author of the LaStanza Series of New Orleans
crime novels and the true-crime book,
SPECIFIC INTENT.

"Gina Gallo's unwavering voice, bubbling from the hellish underground of criminality, reminds us just how much we owe to law enforcement. We wouldn't-want to be in Gallo's shoes, but glomming on to the details secondhand is riveting."

G. Miki Hayden, Murderous Intent Mystery Magazine,
PaintedRock.com

10

Table Of Contents

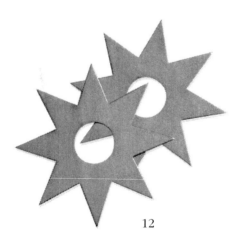

12

"For many of us, a crime scene is a detached event that we only witness as a media audience. The details we're given by a blank-faced reporter are usually missing some of the critical story elements: not just what happened, but why, and how. Questions that remain unanswered for all but those who commit the crime and the cops who investigate it. In Gina Gallo's CRIME SCENES, we're taken behind the ominous yellow tape that cordons off a crime scene for an eye witness view. Gallo's book offers not only a cop's-eye perspective, but that of the victims and perpetrators as well. In a compelling selection of stories, CRIME SCENES takes the reader on a unique tour through the Police experience that begins with the job, takes you to the streets, the victims, and the crimes. It's a walk on the crime side where, for cops, there are no easy answers and no simple truths.

In the world according to Gallo, the only way to define a hero depends on who's keeping score. Her stories are sometimes poignant, sometimes funny, always unflinchingly honest.

Gallo's columns and stories appear regularly in both Blue Murder Magazine and PoliceOne.com. Now, through this impressive collection of stories, she allows us to appear at the crime scene where all our questions can be answered."

David Firks / editor
Blue Murder Magazine
www.bluemurder.com

Forward

Sometimes it sounds like fireworks. But then you realize that those loud repeater blasts followed by screams are actually gunfire, and a crime's just been committed. Other times, there's no noise at all. Silence can be as much a portent as a screaming woman, that bone-chilling quiet that descends after the fact. Crimes are committed in many different ways for just as many reasons. Some of them will be reported in the morning papers, others are simply filed away once the police investigation is complete.

CRIME SCENES was written from a view on a cop's side of the badge. Want to know what it's like to face a gun- one that's held by a little girl? Or to do an undercover narcotics buy that goes horribly wrong? These are real stories about real cops who face down the demons and sometimes are haunted by a few of their own. In a cop's world, there are no tidy endings. Sometimes you don't catch the bad guy, other times, you *are* the bad guy, and always, there's the possibility that you won't make it home again.

This isn't a book about heroes. These are regular

people, cops and the citizens they serve, all living in a world where the rules keep changing and the odds keep shifting, not always in their favor. A world where everyone feels the same fear and confusion, the same pain and rage regardless of who wears the badge.

Any cop can tell you what comes with the job besides a paycheck and a pension. The years and tears and endless parade of images beyond imagination take their toll, break his heart with every crime scene he couldn't prevent, each victim he couldn't save. And even after his career has ended, those faces and stories remain with him, the ones he found behind that crime scene tape. These are some of those stories. Enter at your own risk.

Gina Gallo
www.gallostories.com

16

The Job

GINA GALLO

"....here's some statistics for you all to think about. By the time you finish your Academy training, only about 65% of you will still be here. Some will drop out, some will wash out, some won't be able to take the stress....for those of you who DO make it, some will be promoted to higher ranks.

Some of you may spend your entire career in a beat car. Of those who do manage to make it out of here, 25% won't live to retirement age.

Some of you will be shot, stabbed, and most of you- if you're out there doing your job, can expect your share of broken bones along the way.

And, from every recruit class, a few of you will get killed in the performance of duty. That's the way it is on this job. Get used to it. For those of you who can't, get your ass out right now. Walk out that door the same way you came in."

Opening remarks to the Chicago Police
Academy
Recruit Class,
Orientation Day,   June, 1982

17

The Insane Fish

It has nothing to do with seafood. And like most cop legends in Chicago, everyone's got a different version of how it started. Some say the Insane Fish was the brainchild of beat cops intent on screwing over Internal Affairs. Others think it's a term coined by Marine Unit members who wanted a cool name for their golf league T-shirts. The rest of us are willing to acknowledge the 14th District tactical unit as the original founding Fish.

In a city that has over two hundred gangs, the 14th District has more than its share. The Spanish Gangsters, Insane Unknown and Children of Satan are just a few of the gangs that provide equal opportunity crime. While membership may vary according to location or ethnic group, most gangs favor names that pledge allegiance to Satan, hint at royalty and/or are a testimonial for mental illness. As often as new factions spring up, the hardest part is keeping score.

At the local cop watering hole one night, tac officers Trafford and Danovich tried to figure it out.

"Went through my court log for last period,"

Danovich noted. "Out of all the gang arrests, twenty of 'em were some kind of devils or demons, nine were Kings, Counts or Lords, eighteen were gangster something-or-others, and all the rest were insane. Insane Unknown. Insane Cobras. Insane ViceLords. Like they're poster boys for some asylum, fer Crissakes. How come it's cool to say you're nuts?"

"I know what you mean," Trafford agreed. "Remember those girls we stopped last week? Four thirteen-year olds who called themselves a gang. 'Sisters of the Insane.' What the hell is *that?*"

"Probably what *my* sisters were called when we were growing up." Danovich sipped his suds. "Only back then, anybody called you a nut to your face got the shit kicked out of him."

"Amen to that," toasted Cypher, the cop on the next stool. "The good old days, when things made sense."

"I lock up one more 'banger who belongs to some 'Insane' set, I think I'll go nuts myself," Danovich continued.

"You're halfway there already. It'll be a short trip." Winking, the bartender set down another round. "Don't think any of you guys are wrapped too tight. Maybe you're crazier than they are."

"Fuckin' A!" Trafford chortled. "And there's more of us than them!"

"Fuckin' A!" Up and down the bar, glasses were

raised in toast.

"They may be swimmin' in the pond," someone slurred. "But it's OUR pond, and we're the baddest mothers in it!"

"Hell, yes!" Danovich drained his glass. "Biggest fish in the pond!"

"The Blue Fish!" someone yelled.

"*INSANE* Fish!" shouted another. "Insane Fish rule!"

"Fuckin' A!" Danovich thumped the bar. "We're the Insane Fish! Biggest and baddest in the pond."

It was a joke that got funnier with each beer, but the name stuck. From that night forward, the tac officers of 14 were the Insane Fish. They left memos to each other initialed 'I.F.' Developed their own secret handshake and 'gang sign' in parody of the 'bangers they locked up. Growled "Fish rule!" from the loudspeakers of tac cars passing on the street. It was just a joke, something to laugh about through the course of their watch. And like most cop jokes, it spread throughout the department.

"Heard anything about a bad new gang setting up?" Trafford inquired of his unit commander, affecting a serious tone. "Intelligence we've gotten so far is that these guys are some major bad-asses. Wanna take down the whole damn district." The commander *hadn't* heard of the Insane Fish, but took it under advisement. And when a raw haddock was found, rotting under the front seat of his personal car, he

21

considered it a sign. A blatant attempt by this new gang to intimidate the police, he figured. And sent out a memo the very next day, apprising the Gangs Unit of this latest development. The people in Gangs thought he was one tuna short of a salad.

But the Insane Fish were hitting the streets in a big way. What was the point of being a gang if you couldn't spread the word? The 14th district tac guys decided it was time to stir up the pond.

Cruising through the 'hood one night, Trafford and Danovich spotted a couple Imperial Gangsters lounging on the corner.

"Yo, homes," called Danovich. "Heard a new set's about to take over your turf. Got the guns, got the finest bitches, gonna put you outta business. Whatcha think about that?"

"I think you're nuts, man!" scowled one of the 'bangers.

"Bingo!" chuckled Danovich.

"Insane Fish!" Trafford told them. "Better watch your back."

Other cops dropped hints while doing the paperwork after their arrests.

"What set you run with, man?" they'd ask the sullen gangbanger.

"You know what I am, man. I been arrested like twenty times before."

"You ain't Insane Fish, are you?"

"Insane Fish? Never heard of 'em."

"You will."

"You crazy, man. These Fish, what are they? A Black gang? White?"

"They're EVERY color, bro. A friggin' rainbow gang. The Fish are some bad mothers and they're gonna take you down."

Within a week, the gangs of the 14th District were on full Fish alert. *Nobody* was going to take them down, especially not some newcomers with a wimpy name like Fish. What kind of gang name was that?

News of the Fish spread citywide. Although our department has approximately 12,000 members, word travels fast. Every cop out there could relate to it. As the biggest fish in the pond, we routinely swim in troubled waters. The Insane Fish were ready to shake up the bottom feeders. Those of us who work the street—either beat cars, tactical, or gang cops— anyone who wears the badge was counted as a member. All of us thought it was a hoot.

In the Deuce— the tough 2nd District and home of the brutal Robert Taylor housing projects—street cops drew fish outlines on the grimy windows of abandoned cars. Area gangs who discovered the 'gang symbol' viewed it as the first step of a hostile take-over and hastily scheduled a council of war. Whoever these damn Fish were, *wherever* they were, it was going to be a vicious battle.

After that, there was an outbreak. All around the city, random acts of fishiness were being committed daily by this anonymous new gang. And because the police department brass, like the street gangs, had no clue regarding the Fish's real identity, they were just as concerned.

Memos started to fly through Department mail, all of them pertaining to the vicious upstarts. The Chief of Patrol wanted all available intelligence on the Insane Fish. The Training Academy Director questioned the Research and Development Unit as to whether Fish information would be included in the next Gang Crimes Training Seminars. One of the Assistant Deputy Superintendents thought the Fish posed a hollow threat. Assuming that they were surly vegetarians, he said, "How violent can they be if they don't eat meat? Probably a bunch of wimps who eat quiche and toss water balloons."

Internal Affairs launched a covert investigation of the Fish phenomenon following a frantic phone call from a north side district commander. He'd found a huge, hideous carp's head propped on the seat of his private office toilet, an act he *might* have considered just an odd coincidence except for one thing. In the carp's mouth was a cigar—his preferred brand—and scrawled on the seat, an ominous message:

"You shit with the fishes."

After twenty-two years on the job, the Commander

recognized a warning when he saw one. It meant only one thing—that the Insane Fish had somehow infiltrated the Department. If they were able to breach his inner sanctum, who knew where they'd strike next? These maniacs had to be stopped.

Across the city, street cops were embracing their status as Insane Fish. Some proud members even began to display their membership in cryptic ways. Small fish outlines were found scribbled in the corner of arrest reports. The daily stacks of citations sent to Traffic Court now displayed phantom fish signs along with vehicle description and license plate number. Fish tie tacks appeared on uniform ties, fish T-shirts on tac and gang cops.

Noting the small fish outline on one officer's shirt, a watch lieutenant told him, "I like to get in a little fishing myself when I get the chance. Rainbow trout and bluegill, mostly. How about you?"

"I don't catch fish. I AM fish," replied the cop as he headed for the tac office.

The lieutenant turned to the desk sergeant.

"What the hell did that mean? Is that guy another stress disorder or what?"

"I seen a lot of those fish signs lately." the sergeant shrugged. "I think it's a religious thing. Ya know, like the loaves and the fishes Jesus passed out? Maybe these guys been hanging out at the Chaplain's ministry."

On the city's southeast side, disgruntled drug dealers found fish symbols spray-painted on the doors of their dope houses. They were not amused. Those fishy bastards were moving closer, they told each other. Time to take some offensive action. But it was hard to take *any* action against an invisible enemy.

The Fish follies continued. And, as happens with most large gangs, splinter factions began to form. After work one night, some 4th District cops had a few beers and a major epiphany. Although they'd always be loyal Insane Fish, why not distinguish themselves from the rest? It would be their own South side chapter. Glasses were raised in unanimous approval. Two or three or six beers later, they came up with their chapter name: the Smelts of Satan.

Not to be outdone, other districts followed with their own chapter names.

The 23rd District's Avenging Alewives, the Mo-fo Mackerels of 15, and the Blowfish Blues from 7 were some of the more inspired titles, and the few remembered after the stewed Fish sobered up. It didn't matter. It wasn't chapters or names that were important, only the morale boost that the Insane Fish provided.

It made us a family again. Proud to be part of the team, brothers and sisters who watch each others' backs. A concept they taught us back at the Academy, one that sometimes fades with the reality or the politics of the job.

Almost twenty-five years after it began, the Insane Fish concept is still going strong. These days, new recruits are regaled with Fish war stories from Day One at the Academy, where grinning instructors demonstrate our 'secret gang sign.' It's about family, they tell the recruit classes. Insane Fish are our Police family.

And what would a family be without the occasional prank—hijinks usually aimed at the senior members? Or, in this case, those that carry the most rank.

Like the Area Chief who arrived unexpectedly in the Twelfth District one morning and announced an impromptu roll call inspection. One during which he lumbered along the rows of assembled officers, nastily writing up each one for minor infractions like unpolished shoes, a non-regulation pen in the regulation uniform pocket, or hair that curled over the collar. All bullshit charges, the day watch later agreed. Boss's busy work to justify his salary. A hostile display definitely not in keeping with the brotherly Fish philosophy. Partnered together on Beat 1212, Wade and LaCloche couldn't agree more.

"Guess the chief was really proud of himself," Wade told his partner. "Wrote up a few coppers, now they'll give him some more gold braid for his friggin' uniform."

"Probably the only thing that makes him cream.

Bet he had to change his underwear afterward."

Spotting the Chief's immaculate new car gleaming in the district lot, the two cops smirked. It was time to make a statement in the name of Insane Fish everywhere.

They headed toward their beat, which included Fulton Market—a bustling hive of meat houses, fish markets, and the shipping docks of the finest food purveyors in the city.

Pulling up to the rear dock of the Seven Fathoms Fishery, LaCloche smirked.

"Nice car the chief had, doncha think?"

"A fucking gem," Wade agreed. And waved to the dock manager who approached their car.

"How ya doin', Vito? Whatcha got that's good today?"

"Depends on who it's for," grinned the short mustached man. He'd known these cops for ten years and recognized that look.

"A special friend," Wade replied. "So damn special he wears gold braid up his ass."

"This friend of yours—he'd like something special, or *deluxe?*" Vito pointed to a row of sealed waste buckets.

LaCloche frowned, considering. "Deluxe, I'd say. How 'bout it, Wade? Wouldn't you say he's a deluxe kinda guy?"

"Fuckin' A. He's a deluxe motherfucker if I ever

saw one!"

Vito nodded.

"Those first three buckets—mostly fish heads and guts. Next two are old product—wasn't shipped on schedule and now it's spoiled. But those four on the end..." Shaking his head, Vito rolled his eyes. "That's the shipment from a truck with a blown refrigeration unit. Our loaders opened that truck, two of 'em passed out from the stink. A smell bad enough to be a deadly weapon!"

Wade nodded judiciously.

"That'll work, Vito. Exactly what we need."

"Whatever you want, guys. How many you need? One bucket or two?"

"Two buckets, Vito. This is definitely a two bucket kinda guy."

Heading back to the district parking lot, LaCloche shook his head.

"Two buckets is a LOT. One woulda been plenty."

"One for the front seat, one for the back." Turning smoothly into the alley, Wade drove around to the rear of the lot. "We're making a statement, remember."

Just ahead was the chief's car, shining like a precious jewel.

"Fuckin' A!" grinned LaCloche.

They reached for the buckets. Insane Fish rule.

Blood Brothers

It wasn't just the uniform. Although, staring into the mirror at his brand new blues, the rookie acknowledged a rush of excitement. He was 'The Man' now, impressive in his knife-creased slacks and the blue shirt with the department patches and the silver star, the one they'd given him when he'd sworn to serve and protect. The new Beretta snugged tightly into his breakaway holster was further evidence of his authority, his commitment to enforce the law and keep the peace. Finally he was a cop, after years of dreaming, and months spent sweating through the grueling Academy training program. Adjusting his gunbelt slightly, he struck a self-conscious pose. He was one of the brotherhood now.

Walking into roll-call on that first day, he tried for the correct demeanor. Not quite a swagger, more of an authoritative stroll that meant he was confident, a tough cop ready for anything. And when he was partnered with Hudson, a salty vet with twenty years experience, he did his best to match the older officer's laconic smirk and fathomless eyes. Street cops maintained a game face, he knew. It was important not to show your feelings, allow nothing to crack your tough veneer. Now that he was one of them, he wanted more than anything to be accepted as a good cop, a hard worker, a stand-up guy.

Hudson was amused by the new kid, by his squeaky-clean blues and the eager way he drank in everything. Rolling down the streets of their beat that day, he listened to the rookie's interminable questions, meant to sound like a seasoned cop, he knew, but sounding mostly like an excited kid. Like the green kid that he was. Recalling his own rookie days, Hudson suppressed a smile. He'd been like this, too, in the beginning. He remembered how important it had been to look tough, sound tough, a young pup striving to be a salty old dog. And because of that, he shared some war stories with the rookie, expounded on his views of policing in an ongoing monologue as their beat car nosed through the quiet streets.

"Partners stick together," Hudson told him. "No matter what else happens, that's the bottom line. I got your back, you got mine. That's the first rule of the streets. The *most important* rule."

There were other rules, of course, but all of them centered on taking care of each other. Ending each tour of duty the same way you started it—alive, and intact. Every day you got to go home was a victory.

"We back each other up," Hudson said. "When it hits the fan, you better be there right next to me. That's what we do. First time you chicken out, everybody'll know about it. Then you get a reputation, and nobody will work with you. You get in trouble, nobody'll back you up. Which, out here, is suicide. So stay on your toes, and remember to cover your ass, and mine too. Long as you do that, you'll be okay."

The rookie nodded vigorously, feeling a quick surge of pride. He knew all about the code of the brotherhood, knew he would never violate it. He'd waited all his life to be a cop. Never would he let Hudson down, or anyone who wore the badge.

As that day passed, and the next, and in the weeks that followed, the rookie was determined to prove his worth to Hudson, to the rest of his co-workers, and especially to himself. He fidgeted through the minor jobs—the lost persons, old ladies complaining about their loud neighbors, and waited for the hot calls so he could show his stuff.

A simple domestic disturbance? No such thing as 'simple,' the rookie knew. He entered those calls boldly, ready to disarm the combatants, place himself at the forefront of the altercation to prove he had the heart and guts of a warrior. Disorderly conduct? The offender might be armed, or ready to fight....might even be the look-out for some other criminal action going on near-by. With wary eyes and yearning heart, the rookie steeled himself for the action that never came.

It was during the second month of duty that the call came.

"Disturbance at the store," the dispatcher told them. As Hudson drove toward the specified location, the rookie squirmed impatiently.

"I know that store," he told his partner. "Maybe it's an armed robbery."

Shifting his ever-present toothpick placidly, Hudson barely spared him a glance.

"If it was a robbery, they'd *say* robbery, kid. This is just a disturbance. Maybe one of the customers thinks they ain't gettin' the sale price."

The squad car pulled up in front of the place- a women's clothing store in the middle of the block. Before Hudson could heave himself out of the car, the rookie was on the sidewalk, uniform hat in place, a textbook picture of the correct police demeanor. He had just enough time to glimpse his reflection in the display windows before a youngish blonde male in a leather jacket barreled through the double doors. Catching site of the rookie, he stopped short, and then bolted down the street.

Another man rushed out of the store, the heavy-set store owner who screamed at the rookie.

"Go get that bastard!" he shouted. "Kill him! What

are you waiting for?"

It was all the rookie needed. He raced after the offender, who by now was nearly a block away. Struggling to maintain a visual on the leather jacket that bobbed through the crowds, he flew down one block, then three, then six. After that he stopped counting, just concentrated on keeping his focus. It was up to him to catch the bad guy. Hudson was quite a distance behind him, he figured. But he was younger, fitter from his months of training at the Academy, and he didn't mind picking up his partner's slack. That's what brothers did—what teamwork was all about. It was the moment of truth he'd been waiting for—an opportunity to do what *real* cops do.

The rookie was getting winded. Judging by the erratic weaving pattern his suspect moved in, he was tired too. And when he ducked down the subway stairs, the rookie knew he had him. The blonde man hesitated near the lower stairs, turned halfway as the rookie began his descent. Breathing heavily, the man held up his hand and brought it to the zipper of his jacket.

It was that critical moment, the rookie knew. The one they'd talked about at the Academy, where the scenario plays out and your life hangs in the balance. The split second where instincts and reflexes kick in to decide your fate, define you as a cop, a survivor... or a casualty.

The rookie didn't hesitate. His gun was out almost before he realized it, spitting a stream of fire and death that sent the blond man crashing to the ground.

Later, it would seem like a moment frozen in time. He would remember thinking that his partner would be proud, how the guys in the station would applaud his bravery under fire. He'd faced down a gunman, cheated his own death and delivered another's. He even imagined how the detectives in the follow-up investigation would show him the man's weapon that had almost been drawn, had almost ended his own life.

Except there was no weapon, only the reproachful look of a seventeen year old boy whose life seeped away in spreading pools. In those final moments, he stared at the rookie, held his horrified eyes as he removed what nestled inside his jacket.

It was the sweater he'd shoplifted, a cheap green pullover now sodden with his blood.

His lips moved futilely, rasping out a final message that was hard to hear over the approaching sirens.

"You didn't have to shoot me. I would've given it back."

Stiffed

It's not a job for the faint-hearted. In this city, where the paddy wagon, also known as "squadrol," is used for prisoner transport, as an ambulance and for dead body removal, it takes a certain type of cop to handle the job. While the rest of Chicago's finest patrol a beat, go undercover and fight crime in a variety of ways, the wagon men (and women) are required to do just three things: drag, bag and tag.

It's not unusual for a wagon crew to finish lunch, and then get an assignment like: "Suspicious smell in the house." Which usually means somebody's dead, and has been long enough for the resulting stench to defoliate most of the neighborhood. It's the wagon guys who'll be sent to the river to fish out the floating corpse. And after the detectives are done investigating a crime scene, it's the wagon guys who scoop up the remains and trundle off to the morgue.

A thankless job, some say, but it does have its perks. Very few wagon men are shot by irate corpses. Hardly ever will a citizen flag down a paddy wagon and ask for a ride. Since the presence of one usually means a trip to jail or the morgue, most people keep a respectful distance away.

And there are some other benefits. Although the Department specifies that dead bodies should be transported to the morgue, most funeral parlors tip cops handsomely for "direct delivery." This saves them the trouble of sending out their pick-up crew, and maintains friendly police relations.

Any experienced wagon man can tell you the going rates for city mortuaries, and which of them is their preference. Usually, their choice will have no bearing on location. It doesn't matter whether the mortuary is in their assigned district, or on the other side of the city. For an extra ten or fifteen bucks, they're willing to go the distance. What's a few miles? Nobody's in any hurry, least of all their passengers.

One December morning in one of the North side districts, Axelrod and DeVore had just climbed into their wagon.

"Got one to start off the wagon this morning. Check the man in the east alley, Charleston at Oakley Street. Citizen's calling it in, says he's been there awhile."

They could almost hear the dispatcher grin. *"Hope you haven't had your breakfast yet, guys."*

Axelrod merely shrugged.

"How bad could it be?" he asked his partner. "It was four degrees last night. If this guy's dead, he's a bumsicle. Can't thaw in this cold."

DeVore nodded. Posthumous pick-ups were

37

definitely easier in the winter.

They found their subject in the alley, bluish fingers still curled around an empty pint bottle.

"H.B.D.," Axelrod said, employing the wagon man's technical police term for 'He Be Dead.' "Probably the booze that killed him. That stuff could melt the rust off submarines."

DeVore examined the body. By his estimation, the man had been in his early seventies. No wounds, no evidence of foul play, and no identification. By department policy, another John Doe for the morgue. But Axelrod and DeVore had their own policy.

Thirty minutes later, they were making their delivery to Bondurant's Memorial Chapel, located on the far southeast side of the city, near the Indiana steel mills. At thirty-five dollars per wagon man, they were one of the highest paying mortuaries in the city. Squinting at his newest delivery, Julius Bondurant scowled. He never accepted indigents, or anyone without a family or an insurance policy that would pay handsomely for his services.

"Does he have a family?" he asked.

"Absolutely," Axelrod lied. "We made the notification before we came. They asked us to bring him here."

"Looks like a bum to me."

"He was out there overnight. Had a little Alzheimer's, they said. Must've got lost on the way home from the tavern. It's their grandpa."

"Hmmmmm."

"Name's Babbalucci. Spattafore Babbalucci. They called him Grandpa Spats."

Julius looked suspicious. "He have any ID on him?"

"We had to leave it with the family," DeVore improvised. "The granddaughter just fell apart. Said she'd wait for her husband the lawyer to bring her down here. Too upset to drive herself."

The magic words. Lawyers meant big money. Julius could barely suppress his greedy smile. He counted out seventy dollars to the wagon men who went off whistling. And because business was slow that morning, he instructed his staff to begin work on Grandpa Spats immediately. By the time the family arrived, he'd have the finished body in the cooler and an itemized bill to present.

When the Babbalucci family hadn't arrived by noon, Julian figured they got caught in traffic. Or possibly lost, a common occurrence with those not familiar with that part of town.

Between the steel mills and the smelting plants, with heavy equipment trucks shuttling in between, it was easy to get confused and take the wrong turn off the Dan Ryan Expressway and end up in Hammond.

By late afternoon, Julius was beginning to worry. Grandpa Spats was finished and chilling, and still no family members had shown up or even called. Eight hours was plenty of time. His big mistake was not getting the family's contact information, or even the beat number of those wagon men. Last time he ever trusted *them*.

By noon the next day, Julius was furious. Grandpa's family was a no-show and there was no phone book listing for Spattafore Babbalucci or any name remotely similar. By now he had to face the truth—that he'd been stiffed out of seventy dollars, *and* had a perfectly preserved body in the cooler that was all stitched up with no place to go. He wasn't in the habit of providing free shelf space for deceased indigents, space reserved for the paying customers. Nothing to do but cut his losses, and his "guest" list.

When he ordered his staff to dispose of Grandpa Spats, they were perplexed. Marlon, the newest employee, simply stared. He was pretty sure dragging dead bodies through the city streets wasn't part of his job description.

"Where we s'posed to take him, boss?" Otis, the senior assistant inquired. "Morgue won't take him, not after he been here. Ain't like we can dump him on the street. You can get tickets for littering when it's just an old coffee cup—don't wanna think about what it'd be for a whole body!"

"Why not call the police to come get him?" Alphonse suggested.

"Idiot! It was the cops who brought him here in the

first place! They made me for seventy bucks—you think they're gonna come back?" Julius was livid. "I don't care what you do with him, just get him out of the damn cooler. Costs money to refrigerate that thing, and if he doesn't pay, he can't stay."

In the end, Alphonse and Otis came up with an equitable solution. While they moved Grandpa Spats out of the cooler, they instructed Marlon to select some clothes from those removed from past customers. Something reasonably clean with not too many bullet holes.

Dressed up in his almost new finery, Grandpa Spats looked like a new man. The orange sport coat gave him a rakish look, especially when paired with the green checked golf pants.

"Gloves?" Otis debated. "Or is that too much?"

Busy propping up the body at the corner card table, Alphonse paused to consider.

"Maybe just that purple neckerchief. Jaunty, but not over the top."

Later, the three assistants at Bondurant's Memorial Chapel agreed they'd never had a better fourth for their card games. Spats never cheats, never tips his hand and always keeps a poker face. Six years later, he's still in the mortuary's back room, propped up at the card table, a reminder of Julius' bitter lesson: let the embalmer beware.

Dance with the Devil

Strange thing about fear. It has a special taste—like dust, or sweat, or blood that runs cold when you realize this night might be your last. A familiar taste on my palate but tonight it's worst. I have a date with the Devil. Will be held in the arms of Diablo himself, stare into his demon eyes and hope that somehow I'll get away intact...and alive. But it doesn't seem likely.

So how did I get a date with this demon? Cunning, hard work and a ravenous hunger. In the circles in which I move, he's the prize, this Diablo, the brass ring everyone wants. Tonight, if the fates are kind, I'll get him, preferably before he gets me. This time, I'll leave my weapons at home.

We rendezvous at midnight—prime time for the Dark Prince. I arrive first, hurry through the thick scarred doors and into the inner sanctum, or whatever they call this room where dread and fear hang as heavy in the air as the filmy blue smoke. Blue smoke, black walls and an eerie red glow that shows me the others huddled here in these shadows. I've never been to this club before, but it's the usual scene. Hot jazz from cool dudes on the bandstand oozes through the room. Here, everyone is a nameless face—the best way to hide a past, or ensure a future. But nobody else is in danger tonight. The Devil is coming for me.

In the dark, it's hard to navigate through the sweating hordes. Bodies jostle together but eyes remain shadowed. Fear is the language spoken here. With no windows to vent the hot and fetid air, I can smell that fear as sharp and pungent as my own. Feel the same dread, the same grim knowledge. Death and Diablo usually travel together. Will I be the sacrifice tonight?

I'm ready for whatever comes. Prepared as much as one can be for what might be my last night. Dressed to thrill in blood red silk deep as the heart of darkness that exposes my pale skin and ripe promise—both of which might be broken tonight. He can do that. Diablo is a greedy devil who uses his powers to suit his needs. His desires will orchestrate our dance, but it's my needs that brought me here, and keep me waiting in this fetid pit.

But even in this darkness I know that there are angels among us. No undercover cop works without backup, and mine are at this bar tonight, lurking in the shadows. But I'm the designated bitch who is the offering, the bait who'll talk the talk. Waiting for the man who calls himself Diablo to walk through the door.

I slip onto a bar stool and order a drink. The smudged glass is a handy prop that makes this all seem normal, just another part of a day in the life. No cops come to these parts, so tonight I've got to play someone else. The bartender winks at me. And wipes his hands on the damp apron that conceals his 9 millimeter Glock and two extra ammo clips. My back-up comes heavily armed.

Tonight I have five of them here, strategically placed and waiting, but I've got to dance to the music alone. Tonight my role is a goddess of greed who'll court the devil's favors. It's drugs I'm after, kilos of heroin and coke from one of the most treacherous drug dealers in the country. Diablo is his name, a mortal man as skilled in the Devil's deeds as Lucifer himself. The blood of countless victims stains his hands.

His head count of homicides is daunting even in the ruthless world of hard drugs and cold murder. Diablo's appetites feed on power. Bad blood and cunning are part of his game plan, deceit and cruelty his usual M.O. His enemies are legion but few will take him on. Nobody is willing to battle this demon, but tonight we'll do the dance.

A chill precedes him into the room. Or maybe it's fear that's raising the hair on my neck, squeezing my heart with icy claws. A fitting prelude for the figure who steps out of the murky dark. The Devil wears Armani suits and drinks his bourbon neat.

"Another drink?"

My glass is still untouched but I smile and nod. And stare into eyes that glow like sulfur in his sin-dark face.

"Waiting long?" He doesn't care. Poses the question only as a meter to gauge my apprehension.

"No. Not very."

"Good." And then he smiles. A blaze of porcelain white slashes his lean cheeks where dimples wink improbably. Warms those sulfur eyes to the burnished gold of fine brandy. I realize, belatedly, that the Devil is a babe.

We chat. Typical bar talk bordering on flirtation, but this time, there's an edge. He knows what I want. And I know he's determining just what it is he wants to give me. A tongue down my throat or a knife in my back? Either choice would suit him. The way his eyes crawl like sucking leeches across my breasts tells me he hasn't yet decided.

The bartender lumbers past us, swiping a thin damp rag down the length of ebony surface. The music is slower now, the melody indistinct, or maybe obscured by the tribal rhythms of my pounding heart. Which nearly vaults out of my chest when Diablo touches my arm.

"Pretty," he muses, stroking the pale skin. His

touch is searing. Smooth. Unexpectedly sensual. A minor seduction in this tense scenario. But of course, it's only me who's nervous. The Devil has done this dance before. Long fingers, carefully manicured, glide up to the wild pulse that jars my throat.

"So soft," he murmurs. "I like that." Down the bar, my guardian angel scowls.

More talk. More silky touches. My head is spinning from the heat and heavy sweetness of cigar smoke. Cubans, the only kind Diablo smokes. Another weapon in his limitless arsenal meant to disorient his victims, his partners in the dance.

It's taken a year to get here, this dark bar where a handsome man blows perfect smoke rings and feels my thigh. Twelve months of street surveillance, gathering intelligence on this demon who nuzzles my neck. He smells of bourbon and subtle cologne, and the blood of those who came before me. His ruby ear stud glints like fire as he leans closer to sniff my hair—or my fear—like a predator gauging his prey.

Fingers trail along my spine, deceptively tender. He's checking for wires and concealed weapons. Diablo is no fool. He runs with the big boys—a family of Nigerian drug dealers merciless in their savage credo: Kill anyone who dares to cross them. When it's only flesh his fingers touch, the Devil smiles. My cover is secure. An unarmed woman in a red silk dress is a suitable partner. The transaction will take place tonight. Drugs for money, the dance in which Diablo and I will trip the dark fantastic.

In previous communications, we'd agreed to the terms of the deal. The price. Quality and quantity. And, most important, the location. Even for a woman who dances alone, my back-up needs a game plan.

Most important in this orchestration is a place that offers my angels a clear view. Where it's easy to maintain visuals and close in once the transaction's been made. Preferably, a place clear of traffic or people who might get caught in the crossfire if gun-play is involved. That's an undercover narcotics cop's wish list, but just like Christmas, it's not what we always get. And tonight, in spite of our previous plans, Diablo has different ideas. Instead of the agreed warehouse nearby, he wants to take me somewhere else. His car is outside, he tells me. A short ride to a private place, somewhere we can be alone. Relax and enjoy our shared interests, mix some pleasure with the business.

Panic spikes like fever when he leads me outside. There's a sleek black Mercedes at the curb, with windows tinted dark enough to conceal whoever lurks inside. No savvy drug dealer travels without a goon squad, and the Devil is no exception. If I get into the car, it's a guaranteed transport to Hell. No chance of survival for an unarmed woman in a tight enclosure, surrounded by brutal thugs high on dope and hormones. I can almost visualize that year's hard work and intelligence going up in smoke as wispy as Diablo's cigar.

No, I tell him. And lick lips suddenly dry as tombstones in what's meant as a seductive gesture. I want to be alone with him. Without his friends, without anyone to disturb us. This will be a private party.

I'm trembling now. Desperately hoping Diablo's greedy business sense will take us to the warehouse, the kilos, and his arrest. Rank cold fear ices my skin, makes my nipples poke against the thin silk of my dress like pointing fingers. Diablo smiles. Hot sulfur eyes spark at what he thinks is my arousal.

My car is already parked at the warehouse, I tell him. We can walk there. Take care of business and then...

Sultry intent hangs in the air, and I lick the Devil's cheek.

His goons will follow behind us, but it doesn't matter. As long as I don't get in the Mercedes, I've got a chance, and my back-up team can move into position.

This pre-dawn hour is murky and hushed, with a seeping damp fog thick enough to swallow us whole. Puffing on his cigar, Diablo leads me down the street. No more tender crooning. His feral face is taut with hunger, ready to devour me. And while I'm wondering if my back-up is in place, he's describing the art of this particular deal...and how he intends to sweeten it. He says he likes his women hot, his sex incendiary. Pain as a prelude to the ultimate, fiery bliss. A primal encounter of animal lust.His voice is thick with it, a deep whiskey rasp. Even in the fog, his eyes glitter fiercely.

They should be right behind me, I think. Five armed men ready to take down the Devil. But I can't turn around, can't hear anything over my own heart pounding. And try not to scream when Diablo grabs my arm.

"A shortcut," he grates, propelling me down an alley. There are trucks parked here, pallets stacked high enough to block the view. Rats scurry among the reeking garbage and broken bottles strewn everywhere. A series of sharp turns, another alley, and I know for certain my backup's been lost. No one can maintain a visual in this labyrinth, exactly what Diablo has in mind. He's ready to begin the dance.

One brutal tug, and my dress is torn away in a shriek of red silk. Eyes flame sulfur hot as the Devil's mouth descends, sinking teeth in tender flesh. Pain and panic have me clawing out, but he shoves me down, brands my neck with his glowing cigar.

Screams—my own or the squadron of demons come to witness this dance?—rise up around us like the fires of Hell. We struggle on the rough concrete, roll across gravel and shattered glass. Seconds? Minutes? An eternity as blood fills my mouth from his relentless blows.

My eye is already swelling, and blood runs hot as he slams against me, howling like a hound from Hell. White hot pain, red rage and one sharp silver streak before black oblivion.

Like anyone who's experienced death, it's the angels I see next. Guns drawn, breathless from running through the maze of alleys, my back-up finds me crumpled in a seeping pool. Thick red oozes from the Devil's inert body slumped beside me. Dead sulfur eyes stare in wide open astonishment at the intensity of our last dance, or the thick shard of glass I buried in his jugular.

God vs. the Inferno

It doesn't get any worse than this. And it never gets any easier, even for the seasoned vets who've seen it all. For those of us who think we've mastered the game face, developed that tough shell that allows us to function no matter how bad the circumstances, it's the burn victims who strip away our last defenses.

Chicago cops refer to them as "crispy critters." An apt image, but more of a "whistling-past-the-grave-yard" irreverence that helps to depersonalize their charred remains, allows you to do your job. The nightmares come later. After your first fire, you'll see them in your dreams, or passing through your field of vision even when you're not asleep. A parade of victims beyond description that linger in your mind, conjuring sensory memories so distinct it's like a surreal replay.

You're back at the scene, with the same acrid smoke, the godawful smell of roasted meat that you know comes from people who had no chance. The fire roars, screams echo in a holocaust of hellish sound. Raw fear prickles your skin as much as the searing heat, coils in your gut like a venomous snake. You're convinced it's only smoke that makes your eyes sting. But all it takes is the first tiny body to be dragged out. He's soot-streaked and dusty with no visible burns. So *young*. And that's when you start to pray, fervent pleas that fuse into a single desperate chant: PleaseGodPleaseGod*PleaseGod*, let him live. For this victim of the noxious smoke, your prayers are futile. You see it in the firefighters' eyes, watch as they remove the oxygen apparatus and gently cover his tiny form.

But there's no time for tears. You're a trained professional, expected to do your job. In spite of this pre-dawn hour, the sidewalks are crowded with citizens come to witness this blazing inferno. Sheets of flame unfurl through every window of the eight-unit apartment building. As firefighters swarm through the billowing black smoke, more engine companies shriek up to the scene.

The body count increases. Some died mercifully quickly by smoke inhalation. Those who didn't are shrouded in blankets. They settle and scorch against bodies still cinder-hot, creating an awful singed wool/burnt meat odor. It's enough to have some of the on-lookers retching behind the police line you struggle to maintain. The others cluster together to pray. Gripping an ancient rosary, one old lady leads the faithful in the timeless prayers, wavering only when another victim is carried out.

"....and lead us not into temptation, but deliver us from evil. Amen."

The prayers echo in your head, mocking this brutal reality. You want to scream, demand to know just who or what it was that delivered the countless victims from *this* particular evil. Who allowed babies to be torched like so much trash, ended lives because of one free-basing cokehead? At times like this you doubt the existence of a merciful God. Heaven or hell? Maybe it's all the same, mixed together in one huge stinking pit here on earth that you wade through each time you pin on your badge. You've dealt with enough demons to know it's likely, and tonight, averting your eyes from the tiny victims, you've seen the angels as well.

You see one now—an apparition?—coming toward you through the smoke. Her hair is haloed by the fire's glare, and her chubby faced smudged with soot. Not more than four years old, you guess. She wanders slowly, dragging behind a cherished toy. It's the Cookie Monster, slightly singed now, more gray than blue, but still gripped tightly in her hand. A frown creases her brow as she negotiates the labyrinth of snaking hoses and shouting men.

But when she sees you, her face melts into a relieved smile. At last, a cop—a figure she recognizes. The one who helps whenever there's trouble. Dragging Cookie Monster through the dirt, she stumbles toward you.

"Find my Mommy." The tiny voice is kitten soft, barely audible above the din, as sweet as her Hershey's kisses eyes. An alligatored strip of blisters covers one arm, but she seems oblivious to the pain.

"Find my Mommy, please." She gestures toward the building, directions to expedite your mission. "She's sleeping. I couldn't find her. Can you help me, please?" It's not just the voice that tugs at your heart, or the way her imploring eyes capture yours. It's the absolute faith she has in you, the designated protector. You're the cop, the go-to guy who can find her Mommy, make everything right again.

"What's your name, sweetheart?"

"Erica."

"Okay, Erica. Can you tell me which apartment you live in?"

"202," she recites, impatient now. "Will you *please* find Mommy? She gets scared when she doesn't know where I am." Her voices wobbles over the next words. "I brought something that's her favorite. But I don't know where she is." Her other hand comes up, the one that's fisted around the plastic statue of St. Jude. *The patron saint of lost causes.*

"If you give it to her, she won't be scared anymore, and everything will okay." She places it carefully in your hand.

"Is that true?"

"Yep. That's what Mommy said."

"Wow, that's pretty amazing. Is it magic?"

While Erica chatters about St. Jude, and magic, and her worried Mommy, you listen intently. And promise her that the firefighters will look for her mother, who must be very proud of such a smart little girl. Then you carry her back to the Red Cross table where there are blankets, and hot chocolate and gentle volunteers who can provide diversion for a frightened child.

You know there were no survivors from the second floor. And that Erica's mother is with the others, somewhere in that row of blankets. So you walk past the bodies, the crowd of gawkers and the murmuring prayer vigil, careful to keep your expression blank. Not hard to do when your head is spinning. It's only when you're in the privacy of your squad that you examine Erica's tiny statue—the soot-stained plastic St. Jude...and you lay down your head and weep.

Flaming Guns

It's one of those cop maxims that are written in stone. There's *nothing* a street cop values more than a good partner. Finding that person who's perfect for you is, in the police world, the equivalent of locating the Holy Grail. Something you'd often heard about but were certain was only a myth.

A good partner is someone you can stand to be with forty hours a week without feeling the need to strangle. This is the guy to whom you've bared your soul, shared your innermost secrets, and your deepest fears, most times without saying a word. He just *knows*. He's been with you in the jaws of death and those long boring stretches so quiet you can almost hear your arteries harden. He's got your back come hell, high water, or investigations by IAD, and you trust him with your life.

With the right partner, working in sync is effortless. You can *sense* what the other's going to do in any given situation, where he'll stand, how you'll cover the room. You both know, before it happens, who plays good cop or bad, who does foot pursuits and who does the kamikaze driving. It might appear spontaneous to the outside observer, but you're a team with a choreographed strategy designed to keep you alive. Trial and error have taught you what works best so you've perfected it to an art form. And, like any art form, there are artists and there are masters. After fifteen years together, partners Smitty and Dutch considered themselves Rembrandts.

They patrolled an area of the 9th District known as Canaryville—an ass-kicking blue collar 'hood with a large Appalachian population. A place Dutch had come to refer to as "Forty Acres and a Tooth." It was here they'd perfected their street repertoire, tough to do in a place where the locals bench-pressed engine blocks just to pass the time. On certain blocks of Canaryville, the male residents were either in prison, on their way, or showing off the tattoos from their most recent stint. Drinking and fighting were the two biggest pastimes, with domestic violence a close second. Throw in a little reefer, a little crank, maybe some engine cleaner to huff, and they were ready to rumble any time. But nothing beat the weekends.

There was a definite pattern to Canaryville weekends. By five o'clock on Friday, most of the gin mills were already packed. Waylon and Willie blared on the jukebox, and platinum blonde barmaids set out coasters large enough to use for pressure dressings if the fights got too bloody.

But first there were the amenities. Beer was the

kick-off drink, followed by shots and beers, and finally straight Kentucky bourbon tossed back neat. A manly drink for the macho men who wore Harley-Davidson caps and remembered to spit their tobacco before sucking face with a Canaryville barfly. By the last call for alcohol, some had fallen in lust and wandered off with their queen for the night. Those who hadn't staggered out sour mash stupid and spoiling for a fight. It didn't count as a good drunk unless you whupped somebody's ass. Sometimes it was the guy one barstool over, other times you brought it to the wife at home.

That was usually where Smitty and Dutch entered the picture. When enough furniture had been tossed through windows, or enough ceiling plaster dropped on their heads, irate neighbors called 911. Not to restore the peace, simply to collect the bodies. They figured by that time, someone *had* to be dead.

Fifteen years in "Forty Acres" had taught Smitty and Dutch a whole bag of tricks. They knew that handling Canaryville domestics sometimes required a different technique than others. In most domestics, the combatants fight each other, and sometimes the police. In Canaryville, where bloodletting is a revered sport, they fight everybody. Which is why the two cops decided that the best defense is to be as offensive as possible—without lifting a finger. They call it the "flaming guns" approach. And used it, just last Saturday night, when responding to a call on Union Avenue.

It was a domestic disturbance ranked as high priority since both combatants still had pulses. Upon arrival, the officers discovered that the front door was missing from its hinges. Once they got a load of Earlene and Cletus, the happy couple, they couldn't decide if he'd kicked it in or she'd removed it so her ass could wedge through the three foot opening. Smitty and Dutch had seen big people before, but these two were behemoths. Once they got past the glare from Cletus's bowling ball head, they noticed the tattoo across his chest: "Born to Ride Hogs." Since there was no motorcycle on the premises, Smitty assumed it was a declaration of sexual preference and decided against inquiring further.

Hank Williams Jr. was twanging from the radio—a song called "Whiskey Bent and Hellbound," which, as far as Dutch could see, pretty much summarized the total situation. Cletus had already busted up most of the furniture and was working on the walls. After running through her arsenal of plates and glasses, Earlene was now in iron skillet mode. He was drunk, she was pissed, and both of them were out for blood. And since both cops together barely equaled the size of Earlene's thigh, a forcible approach might not be the most sensible. It was time for "Flaming Guns."

"Worthless sumbitch!" Earlene bellowed. "He been out drinkin' all damn night, then come up in here smellin' like some other bitch, and I'm s'posed to take it? He can kiss my ass!" *Crash!* The deep fryer whizzed past Cletus' ear. "And then he think he's gonna put a hurt on me besides? Y'all better lock his evil ass up 'fore I kill him!" *Smash!* The griddle sailed through what was left of the window.

By now Cletus had lost interest in the plasterboard and was looking for some flesh to rearrange. Smacking a ham-sized fist in his hand, his lips peeled back in a four-toothed snarl.

"Throw one more thang at me, you bitch, I'm gonna tear off both your arms and shove 'em down your big fat mouth!" His head swiveled toward Smitty and Dutch. "And y'all can't do a damn thang t'stop me!"

As the lead-off flame, Dutch stepped forward. Propping one hand on his hip, he gestured, limp-wristed, toward the glaring Cletus.

"May I mention that's a stunning belt buckle you're wearing? I just *love* a Western motif, don't you? That is a stallion, isn't it?" His breathy giggle was followed by a sly wink. "You know what they say about a rearing horse."

Pivoting toward Earlene next, Dutch pursed his lips in a sulky pout.

"And lucky you, Miss Thing! If I had a big stallion

like this in *my* stall, I'd be saddle-sore for days!"

Earlene stopped, mid-toss, to gape at the simpering cop.

Flipping back his blond hair, Dutch sent Cletus a flirty smile.

"But I bet you hear that all the time. A man like you, so...powerful. So *masculine.*"

Dutch's eyelids fluttered dreamily as he heaved a gusty sigh. Hard to do when he was trying not to laugh. Cletus had frozen in his tracks, slack-jawed in astonishment. Where the hell had this crazy cop come from?

"...and the jeans are just perfect. Stone-washed denim, am I right? Although you could carry off the black—a total Johnny Cash thing, y'know?" Tapping a finger against his chin, he scrutinized the flummoxed Cletus. "A mesh tank would be fabulous, too. Something to show off those *incredible* pecs."

"Packs?" brayed Earlene. "Cletus, what the hell is he talkin' about? Packs of *what?*"

It was time for Smitty to step up to the plate.

"You *bitch!*" he shrieked at the fawning Dutch. "You have the nerve to flirt right in front of me? After everything we've been to each other?" Slapping a distressed hand to his chest, Smitty's face crumpled. "Cut my heart out why don't you? After this, it'll never beat again."

"I think this crazy sumbitch's havin' a heart attack!"

Cletus decided. "Damn, Earlene, he's about to keel over on the spot."

"It's nothing," sniffed Smitty, weakly clutching his chest. "Just my...condition. Which is why he doesn't care anymore. Flirts with the every big stud he sees!"

"Such a drama queen!" hissed Dutch. "It's your jealousy that drove me away, not the damned condition!" Tilting his nose disdainfully, he minced over to the far corner.

"Condition? Ain't that like a disease?" Earlene's brows scrunched together while she tried to recall what she'd learned watching Jerry Springer. There were nuts like this on his show all the time.

"Maybe he got one a them fruit diseases! They all get 'em, y'know!" Cletus looked around frantically, wondering if the cops had touched anything. He couldn't remember. Which meant he'd have to swab the whole damn house down with disinfectant, and a back-up of lye soap, just in case.

"I'm feeling a little dizzy," whined Smitty, shielding his eyes with his hand. "This happens every time he does this to me. I can't bear the stress!" Through his fingers, he watched Cletus' bloodshot eyes go wide with terror.

"Hell's bells, Earlene, he's fixin' to pass out. Call 911, tell 'em to send an ambulance!"

"I *did* call 911, remember? They came to lock your ass up."

"They ain't touchin' my ass! In fact, they better not touch anything. They can just walk back out that door."

When Dutch blew him a kiss, Cletus took two steps backward.

"Listen, y'all. We don't need you here. Everything's fine now. Y'all can just go on about your business. Ain't that right, Earlene?" His voice rose desperately at the last question.

His wife was watching the coquettish Dutch with narrowed eyes. She hated when someone flirted with Cletus, even if it was a man. And what kind of man was he anyway, to dump his lover over a little 'condition'? Although maybe Cletus was right. She'd heard such things were contagious. Her glance shifted back to Smitty, checking for any scabs or rash. Or did that only happen with chicken pox?

"Y'all heard my husband," she told the cops. "We 'preciate your comin', but we don't need you anymore. Everything's fine." And moved toward the hulking Cletus in a show of solidarity.

Back in the car, the chortling Dutch radioed the dispatcher with their job code: "One- F." It meant: domestic disturbance, peace restored.

"*Got another one comin' right back at ya,*" the dispatcher said. "*Take a domestic disturbance, 44th and Wallace. Complainant's name is Bohannon.*"

"Ten-four."

63

As the squad car rolled down Union Avenue, Dutch smoothed back his hair.

"Listen, if this turns out to be another Flaming Guns thing, you be the bitch this time."

"I can't be the bitch. I got the mustache." Smitty retorted.

"My throat's gettin' sore for all that whinin'. You can be the bitch one time."

"In your dreams, asshole. I'm the one with the condition."

"Fuck your condition..."

The conversation continued all the way to 44th Street. Flaming Guns ride again.

The Street

BY GINA GALLO

"...When cops refer to the 'streets' they are not referring to Chicago's downtown traffic. The street is a phenomena that's a complex and unique entity unto itself. It has a distinct personality...is a blend of a thousand subcultures that manifests in many forms. It's affected by the morning headlines, the heat of the day, the moon at night, the NBA championship, who just went to jail and who just got out. I once met a policeman from the LAPD who referred to the "street" as "La Puta," Spanish for "the whore." How appropriate, I thought. Lacking in moral rectitude and devoid of any real feeling or compassion. La Puta will give you whatever you want, anyway you want it, but you WILL pay the price."

Lieutenant Dennis Banahan
Area Two
Homicide
March 21, 2000

Mailbox Marilyn

Young cops learn about her early on. In the first weeks of the Chicago Police Training Academy's program, rookies are told about Mailbox Marilyn— stories so absurd, so far-fetched they have to be mythical. Once they hit the streets, these same rookies realize those stories don't even come close to doing her justice.

Among the ranks of Chicago prostitutes, Mailbox Marilyn is a legend in her time. A North side whore, she works various locations as mood and business opportunity dictate. Sometimes North Avenue near Clybourne, sometimes the Broadway stroll. She's not particular about the area as long as business is brisk.

Marilyn has no pimp, which is unusual for a whore who's been out there as long as she has. (A time frame that's indefinite, since Mailbox Marilyn stories have been handed down father-to-son within the Police Department for generations.) Obviously, this is a woman with staying power. Most cops estimate that she's on the downside of 70, although she does-n't look a day over 85. Weighing in at less than 100 pounds, she's best described as a shriveled grandma in search of the Big Bad Wolf—as long as that wolf can pay the price.

There are stories of Marilyn owning a penthouse on Chicago's ritzy Gold Coast, of the children she put through graduate school, one trick at a time. Nobody knows for sure and Marilyn's not talking. She'd rather discuss services and prices, or try to con the local beat cops into buying her coffee when she's been working hard and hasn't had a break.

You wouldn't make her as a prostitute just by looking at her. Not immediately, unless she approaches you with her toothless smile and offers to suck you until your toes curl. At first glance, she appears to be a homeless person, small and wizened, dressed in ragged clothes. She wears no wig, no make-up, none of the flash and trash favored by other hookers. She's simply out there, shuffling along the street, waiting for customers. Judging by her long history of vice arrests, Marilyn's business has always been booming. And that, according to legend, is how she got her name.

Marilyn always favored the early evening trade, often positioning herself outside factories to catch the after-work crowd looking for a quickie before heading home. It was fast, convenient and, for Marilyn, very profitable. So profitable that she usually had a respectable wad of cash before the other girls even hit the streets. And Marilyn knew what every smart street whore knows—that it's never a good idea to carry around a bankroll. She wore no wig in which to stash the cash as other whores did, and had only one place she could think of to conceal it from calculating eyes. She was a prime target—not big enough to fight off the other girls, not quick enough to elude the junkies looking for some fast dope money. Where else to hide the cash but *inside* her? At least in her 'personal vault' she knew her cash was safe. Not many people would think (or have the stomach) to search her there.

Her system was simple. After a certain number of customers, it would be time for direct deposit. Marilyn would remove her gooey bankroll, stroll into one of the many currency exchanges where she was known, and purchase a stamped envelope. And let the U.S. Postal Service provide temporary sanctuary for her funds.

Marilyn is a legend among cops and postal workers alike. Just as police recruits hear her stories in the Academy, new mail carriers are warned in advance to wear gloves when collecting mail on Marilyn's beat. Not hard to guess where she's working, they're told. Just look for a wrinkled old bag lady, a nearby currency exchange and a mailbox with an unmistakable scent.

But somehow, in spite of all the stories and advance warnings, rookie cop Sal Bonaventure was not prepared for his first encounter with the legendary lady—a story that for most of his sixteen-year career has been gleefully recounted by witnesses and co-workers.

At the time, twenty-four year old Sal was fresh out of the Academy and newly assigned to the North side's Fourteenth District. During his first tour of duty on the four-to-midnight watch, he was partnered with Jaime Arrullo, a nineteen-year vet who found the new kid amusing. As they cruised slowly through the late afternoon traffic, Sal rattled on about all the many reasons he became a cop, his noble dreams of helping humanity. The same story Jaime had heard countless times before from green kids in brand new blues eager to be ass-kicking, vinegar-pissing cops just like they'd seen on TV, in between slaying the dragons for a population that depended on the Police to be their heroes and saviors. Chomping on a toothpick, Jaime nodded absently, and decided to give Sal an unofficial tour of the citizens he'd be saving.

Turning the squad car down Division Street, Jaime cruised slowly until he spotted her—the slight, shriveled old lady with the sparse gray hair hobbling out of the currency exchange. Pulling to the curb, he and Sal sat back to watch her stand uncertainly on the corner, clutching her ragged sweater against the wind.

"Lots of homeless people around here?" Sal

inquired.

"She ain't homeless. Just another senior citizen."

"Damn shame that she's out here in such a dangerous neighborhood," Sal said in his best Dudley Do-Right voice. "Old lady like that, anything could happen to her."

And usually does, if she has anything to say about it, Jaime thought. But he only nodded.

"Maybe we oughtta give her a ride home," Sal continued. "It's getting dark out, and the poor thing must be freezing."

She's got ways of keeping warm, Jaime thought, but he smiled at the rookie.

"That's a good idea. Maybe you wanna go ask her. Make her feel special, being helped by a nice young officer like you. Do the uniform proud, y'know?" Exactly the right words to have Sal jumping out of the squad and squaring his uniform hat proudly. Like the official poster boy for Officer Friendly he strode up to Marilyn, full of kind thoughts and good intentions.

While Jaime watched from the car, Sal bowed slightly to the old lady and offered his arm. Too far away to hear the conversation, Jaime could only watch what happened next. Marilyn beamed her patented toothless smile, exposing gums that looked like shellacked rubber. Her rheumy eyes raced down the length of Sal in a practiced once-over. This fine young stud was interested in a ride? This must be her lucky day!

Clutching the young cop's arm, she allowed herself to be escorted back to the squad. When Sal gallantly opened the rear passenger door, she cackled delightedly.

"You're some hot piece, alright!" she crowed, crawling into the back seat. A remark Sal missed, since Jaime was instructing him to get in the back seat with her.

"She's a senior citizen, kid," the older cop reasoned. "Wouldn't want her to bounce around back there and hurt herself."

Sal barely had time to settle into the back seat before Marilyn gave him a preview of coming attractions. Yanking her dress up over her waist, she spread her legs, licked her lips and urged him to take the road less traveled. Sal choked—as much from the shock as the musty smell that filled the car. She had to be crazy. He'd heard about those old folks with Alzheimer's before...but how did he deal with one?

"Uh, ma'am, it's a little chilly. You'll want to cover up before you catch cold."

"Cold? Baby, I can make you sweat blood and piss steam before I'm through," Marilyn promised, diving for his regulation zipper. "Lemme see what kind of piece you're packin', honey!"

In the front seat, Jaime was hysterical. And wondered whether he should assure the new kid that penicillin would probably be covered by his health insurance after a close encounter of the Marilyn kind. He decided that, to commemorate this momentous occasion, it was his duty to capture Sal's experience for the listening pleasure of their entire watch. Keying in the radio mike, he held it aloft, recording and broadcasting to every squad car in the district.

"That's some mighty fine dick!" Marilyn cackled, ducking lower.

"JESUS, lady!" Sal yelped. "For God's sake, keep your hands off me!"

"Don't worry, baby, I can suck the chrome right off Dirty Harry's magnum!"

"Listen, I *said*—"

"First one's a freebie, honey. Police discount."

"Forget it! Don't...hey, wait a minute...CHRIST ALMIGHTY, Jaime, she's tryin' to BLOW me!"

Since there are no handles on the inside rear squad car doors, and a thick steel mesh screen between the front and back seats, Sal and Marilyn were trapped together, screeching over the radio airwaves until Jaime decided to spring his partner. Which, according to his account, was sufficient time for the rookie cop to discover Marilyn's secrets of 'personal banking,' and earn him his co-workers' nickname of "Magnum Force" for the rest of his career.

Loaded for Bear

It was like a wet dream with his eyes wide open. The way they were laid out before him—dozens of them—long, sleek and tempting—he'd never been more aroused. How could he ever choose just one? It was an impossible task, which must be why most guys had two or three, sometimes more. He wanted them all, knew he'd take as many as he could afford. Like most everything else in his life, money could make or break his dreams.

He'd waited a long time for this day. Everyone had, ever since they'd heard it was coming. It was a milestone that separated boy from man, rank recruit from one of the troops. A rite of passage that every cop who wears a badge remembers most—Gun Sales Day. Today they'd purchase their service weapons, and if finances allowed, a secondary one as well.

The Police Academy recruits were herded into a conference room where smiling salesmen waited behind tables lined with state-of-the-art weaponry. The choices were endless. He moved along slowly, scanning the merchandise. Some of the other eager recruits were dry-firing the pistols, something he knew only rank amateurs did. It was tempting, but he reminded himself that he was a professional now, about to go into full uniform. He settled for simply holding the guns, hefting the weight of them, cradling them reverently as he leveled the sights. They all felt natural in his hands, a natural but deadly extension of his arm.

But what to choose? Automatic or semi? Brushed or carbon steel finish? A snub nose was a definite, one he'd tuck into an ankle holster like the old-timers did. He'd heard their stories, how it was a war out there and you had to be prepared. Forewarned was forearmed, they said. He planned on being armed to the teeth. He didn't plan on being a casualty.

In the end, he chose a matte black 9mm that carried death for fifteen enemies. A snub came next, a six-shot blue steel with combat grips. And because it made him feel like Dirty Harry, a .44 Magnum that he couldn't resist. It felt like a cannon in his hand, all brushed steel and deadly promise. The perfect supplementary weapon for the street warrior he intended to be. By that time, his budget was shot to hell, but it didn't matter. There were still a few more paydays before he hit the street, and he planned to buy another gun before then. You couldn't be too prepared.

On his first day at his training district, he was more

than ready. The weight of the guns pulled down on his belt, forcing an awkward rolling gait in order to balance it all. When he lumbered into the squad room for roll call, the other cops nudged each other. This new kid was loaded for bear. Had so much firepower hanging off his brand new gunbelt he clanked when he walked. Privately, they took bets to see which would happen first—his pants would fall down, or he'd trip, accidentally discharge one of those guns and shoot off his foot.

In the squad car, his training officer was more understanding.

"Guess nobody's gonna outgun you, huh?"

Like a veteran of a thousand battles, the recruit nodded seriously. "You never know what's coming at you out here," he said. "I intend to be ready."

The T.O. nodded politely. With all that weight he carried, the kid was getting a total cardiovascular workout with every step he took. Along with the guns, there were his cuffs, extra ammo clips, radio and baton. A steel flashlight hung suspended in between, a canister of pepper spray, a key ring and a leather knife sheath.

"That a Bowie knife you got there, son?"

"In case I run out of ammo."

The T.O. bit back a smile. As far as he could see, the only thing missing was a slingshot and bag of rocks in case they had to bean some advancing marauders. He decided not to mention it though. Better not give the kid ideas. He'd seen enough recruits to recognize the symptoms of 'New Cop Fever.' The pristine uniform, the walking arsenal, the proud swagger that meant they were the roughest and toughest on the street. It didn't last long, usually just until their first reality check. Which, for most of them, happened the first time they had to chase some young, lithe street thug who ran fast as a cheetah in his felony flyers. Hefting thirty extra pounds of firepower didn't seem like such a good idea then. Or the first time they saw a shooting victim. Real life's a hell of a lot different than TV. Witnessing someone's blood seep out made you less anxious to shed it. Watching sightless eyes fade to black underscored how fragile life is.

In the days and weeks that followed, the recruit never dropped his guard. He approached every traffic stop as though it were a ticking bomb. Kept his hand poised on his gun even while answering simple calls, like the irate lady whose begonias had been assaulted by a neighbor's dog. Never let anyone get too close to his 'personal space,' even the lost senior citizen who'd wandered away from the nursing home. As far as he was concerned, vigilance was the key. You never knew where danger lurked.

At the end of his training period, he was assigned to the 4th District on the far southeast side, on the edge of Chicago's city limits. Near the Indiana steel mills, it was a tough blue collar community with a large gang population. The perfect place for a cop like him. He figured that after a year on the street, he'd move up to tactical and then the Gangs Unit. It seemed a logical career progression. He knew some cops were content to work a beat car for the length of their careers, or maybe move to an inside job. For him, that would be a slow death by boredom. He loved being a cop. Loved the excitement, knowing that each night would be different than the one before, and that always, always, danger lurked just around the corner. And more than anything, he loved knowing he was responsible for the public's safety. As their guardian and protector, he was the figure they depended on.

He wasn't going to let them down. He was brave, he was careful, and he was going to make a difference.

It was an ambition that fueled him, earmarked him for what might have been a distinguished career. Something his co-workers and supervisors noticed immediately. This was a kid on the way up. Which, when they heard about it, made the incident that occurred on the morning of May 26th all the more surreal. He was working the second watch then, had started out his morning with a simple disturbance call at a grocery store. It was nothing serious, just an argument between the Croatian grocer and an old woman clearly unhappy with the raised price of produce. After a quick mediation, he was heading back to the squad car.

It was warm that morning, the air almost syrupy with the scent of spring flowers. Still early enough for the birds to chorus from the greening trees. He paused a moment, drinking in the day, the warmth, the morning bustle along the streets. And didn't immediately register the sound of tires screaming behind him, the growl of an engine just before impact. By that time, it was too late.

It was odd, he thought, how the scenario played out in slow motion. How his senses were suddenly more acute, registering each moment with absolute clarity. The sound of his weapons smashing metal against metal. His Bowie knife clattering to the ground. The driver's eyes wide with shock and fear behind the wheel of the careening bread truck. The front of it read, *Heartland Bread and Baked Goods—From our oven to your table with love.*

Amazing how calm he was, crushed between the truck and car. And funny how, when the time came, you *knew*. He couldn't move, couldn't stop the hot red flow.

Felt it clog his throat before he could manage his last words.

"It wasn't supposed to happen like this."

Special Delivery

The Fire Department's paramedics are waiting when we get there. In the projects, they won't get out without a police escort. If the police don't show, they won't go in at all. Today, their red and white rig is parked far enough from the buildings to avoid random shots or hurled bottles, but even so, their heads are swiveling, watching the people who loiter near the entrance. For unarmed professionals who travel with large quantities of drugs, it's a natural reaction. In Chicago, paramedics responding to emergency calls in the inner city are held up almost as often as convenience stores or gas stations.

When our squad car pulls up, they're visibly relieved. It's Davis and Hollub, one of the regular teams we've assisted before.

"Whatcha got this time?" asks Tony, my partner.

"Woman in labor," Hollub yanks open the storage door to gather their gear—the medication box and a folding gurney.

"Should I even ask what floor she's on?"

A faint grin from Davis. "Twelfth floor, man. You *know* nothing ever happens on the lower levels."

Tony barely suppresses a groan. In the projects, the elevators seldom work, and even if they did, police never take them. It's the perfect place for an ambush. The elevator cars are a dead zone where police radios can't transmit. Cops in elevator cars are easy prey for residents who climb to the top and shoot through the car's ceiling, or pour gas on the cables and set them on fire. Either way, we'd be dead meat, which is why all of us use the stairs. And now we're dreading the twelve floor return trek hefting the weight of a pregnant woman.

We start our ascent cautiously. The stairs are dark and narrow, illuminated only by the beam of our flashlights. At any time, sniper shots could be fired from the top of each steep flight. In many ways, the stairwells are just as dangerous as the elevators, often used as garbage dumps, a substitute bathroom, and a convenient disposal for victims' bodies. We pick our way carefully, dead center up the narrow concrete steps, never certain just what or whom we're stepping on. Rats and skittering roaches feeding off the reeking piles barely pause as we approach. On this ninety degree day, the cinderblock walls capture enough heat and stench to rival a backed-up sewer.

By the second flight, we're all sweating. By the fourth, we're wondering about portable oxygen.

"Christ!" gasps Tony. "Shoulda worn a gas mask.

Why didn't you just tell the lady to meet us in the lobby? I thought exercise was good for pregnant women."

"Not if the kid's about to pop out." Hollub pauses, shifting the weight of the gurney. "Just remember to breathe through your mouth."

"And be glad it's not a dead body," Davis adds. "You might be on the lower end of the gurney going down and you know what happens then."

"Shoulda been a damn tool-and-die maker," Tony grumbles, resuming his climb. "My mother warned me but did I listen? Noooooooooo! Make better goddamn money, don't have people shootin' at my goddamn ass, don't have to haul a single goddamn body down a couple million stairs..."

"...and wouldn't have a bunch of cop groupies ready to suck your goddamn dick!" Hollub finishes. "Everything's a trade-off, man."

By the time we stagger onto the twelfth floor, we're ready for our own paramedics. Our soaked uniforms are plastered to us, and even Davis, the avid jogger, is gasping for air.

"Any chance she'd consider a home delivery?" Tony pleads as we follow the paramedics down the dim hall. "Maybe convince her it's earth-friendly—an ecology thing?"

But Davis and Hollub are darting ahead. The apartment door is open, and we can hear a woman's tortured moans.

We find her sitting on the toilet. A yellow sundress is bunched around her massive belly, and her legs splayed wide as she groans.

"JEEEE-ZUZ, Lawd! I can't stand it!" Her face is contorted, slick with sweat, and her eyes filmed with pain. While Hollub snaps the gurney into a chair position, Davis crouches at her side.

"How far apart are the pains?"

"What?" Her hand clamps down, a human vise on his offered arm. "It hurts! God-a-mighty, I'm gonna DIE!"

"You're not going to die. What's your name?"

"Ooooohhhhh!" She squeezes down again, effectively cutting off his circulation. A bitter whiskey smell fills the small bathroom. The labored gasps she's blasting out are at least ninety proof, a sign that she's already tried some alternate pain relief. "It's...Giselle."

Davis manages a soothing voice even though his fingers are turning blue. "Okay, Giselle, we're gonna help you, but you have to help us. Tell me how much time there is between pains."

Giselle pauses, mid-groan, and looks at him like he's lost his mind. "Time? Ain't no time between pains. Just a bad hurt that don't quit."

This is *not* a good sign. No time between pains could mean she's fully dilated, ready to deliver. Tony might get his wish for a home delivery after all. But then we'd have *two* bodies to carry down the stairs.

"And why are you on the toilet?" Hollub inquires, leaning forward to check her vital signs.

This time, Giselle is sure he's just escaped from the puzzle palace. "Why the hell you think?" A belching hiccup, and then, "I'm tryin' to have a bowel movement."

"No you're not," Davis assures her. "It just feels like that when the baby's ready to come out. Don't push."

"Don't push? Are you crazy? I told you—"

"You push any more, that baby might shoot right down the toilet." In one quick move, the paramedics lift her off the commode and onto the waiting gurney.

"But I—" Before she can say another word, Hollub is strapping the safety belts over the mound of her belly.

"Did your water break?"

"Water?" Giselle pauses, confused. And looks around foggily as they wheel the gurney out the door.

"Did you feel a gush of water come from between your legs?"

"Oh, *that*! Yeah, I passed a little water." Her hands grip the side rails as we rush through the hall. "But where y'all takin' me? I *really* have to go to the bathroom!"

"We're going to the hospital," Davis explains patiently. "They'll take care of you."

Giselle looks dumbfounded. "Why come I got to go to the hospital? I can do it at home."

"Home delivery!" Tony hisses to Hollub. "Let's just take her back." Arranging a crocodile smile on his face, he leans toward the indignant woman.

"That's just what I was telling these people, ma'am. You'd rather do it at home, just like the pioneer women did."

"What kinda mess you talkin' about, boy? Them pioneers did it in the woods." She scowls at the four of us as we begin the twelve floor descent. "This really ain't necessary. I *told you* all I gotta—"

"Hey, Giselle! What's wrong, girl?" A neighbor pokes her head around the eleventh floor doorway. "You sick?"

"Hell no, I ain't sick. Just tryin' to take a shit in my own house when these polices come bustin' in..."

The neighbor's mouth drops open. "Y'all lockin' her up cuz she takin' a shit? Is you crazy?" Her voice scales up to a shriek that bounces off the stairwell walls. "These no-good motherfuckers is *arresting* a poor woman using her own bathroom!" A slight pause, followed by the sound of crashing glass. It's a wine bottle the friendly neighbor has lobbed at our heads.

"We got rights!" she screams after us. "Why you got

84

to treat us like animals?"

As point man for the front of the gurney, Davis picks up speed. But it's hard to navigate in the dark, even harder when at least 250 pounds of belly and indignant mother are looming right behind you. Giselle has resumed her moaning, which alarms the other neighbors crowding in their landing doors. They've been alerted by the screams and wails of the first neighbor, who's followed us down five flights like it's the road to Calvary and we're about to martyr the belching Giselle. When they hear of our shameless bathroom abduction, their outraged voices join the din. Soon, more bottles are being tossed, followed by garbage aimed at our heartless heads. Any second now, someone's going to open fire.

Giselle moans louder. While Hollub struggles to keep a grip on the tilted gurney, Davis is dodging garbage, Tony's swearing, and I'm wondering why *all* of us don't become tool-and-die makers. After a call like this, I'm ready to sign up.

It's twelve flights that seem like a hundred. After what must be an eternity, we're almost to the bottom when Giselle bellows like a wounded moose.

"This is *it!*" she screams. "It's coming!"

"Don't push!" yells Hollub, who's in the direct line of fire. "We're almost there!"

But it's too late. Giselle is bearing down, teeth clenched in an animal snarl. Another frenzied scream

85

and then she forces it out—a fusillade of shit that blasts out, covering Hollub, the stairs and the floor below.

"Ooooooo-weeee!" she cackles triumphantly. "What a relief! I been tryin' to do that for days!"

While the dripping Hollub staggers blindly toward the ambulance, the rest of us maneuver through the slippery mess.

"Just don't push," Davis tells the woman. "We'll have you at the hospital in no time."

"I already went to the bathroom. Why I still got to go to the hospital?"

By now even Davis has lost his patience.

"For God's sake, lady, you want to have this baby or not?"

"Baby?" Giselle stares at the three of us now covered in sweat and stinking garbage. "I ain't pregnant." She follows our gaze to her barrel belly. "Just a little constipated, that's all. But I cooked me some cabbage, and it worked like a charm." She burps again contentedly. "I feel a lot better."

"But what about the baby?" Tony asks.

"Oh, you must mean my sister!" Giselle nods proudly. "Yeah, she gonna have that baby anytime now. That's why I called 911. She's upstairs in the bedroom, waiting for you.

"La Puta"

In Spanish, it means "the whore." The best word to describe the woman who's led you in this reckless dance. For twenty years you've courted her, a bitch who sucks you dry even as you wish her dead. But she's irresistible, a siren in slut's clothing that you want still, even now that you know the truth. She doesn't love you. She's never loved anyone. But like most whores, she'll give you anything you want for a price.

It's just business to her, something you knew at the beginning. At the time, you figured you could handle it. Like countless victims before, all you planned to do was use her. Then you fell in love.

You don't remember how it happened. You were young then, dazzled by this mysterious bitch who was hot, dark and more dangerous than you knew. You could almost taste her. Wanted to drink her moans, wondered what would it be like to suck her up, conquer her as no man had before. She coiled around you, whispering the challenge, inviting you to try. That's when the seduction began.

Later, you won't remember when it got crazy, how

you got here, raw and sweaty, scarred by her merciless claws. Some nights she lets you win, some nights she leaves you bloody, but you still can't walk away. It's beyond an addiction, too deep for mere obsession. She's part of you now, who you are and what you've become because of her. This whore is the street. And every night, you pin on the badge and return to her, wondering who wins this time, and who will be left bleeding.

Your thoughts drift back to the beginning. New to the street, you were brash enough to think you could own her. Just like the others who'd tried before and those who were still coming, all with the same intent: to master this bitch you fought and hated, loved and missed after each night was over. Not easy with a heartless whore who shows no mercy.

Each time it was the same. You were lulled by her siren's song—sounds that defined her, pulled you deeper into her dark heart. Exciting sounds that made your pulse trip. No one understands unless they've been there, prowled through her darkness and heard it themselves. A cacophony of sound— screams, thumping boomboxes, harsh laughter fading in the night air. Somewhere, a loud-talking woman, a bitch-slapping man. Gunfire? An every night occurrence—shots and shrieks and the blood that followed.

It was a crash course in Real Life 101, and La Puta was the teacher. Her lesson plan? To fuck you as she had the others. Trying to beat her became the addiction, a relentless Jones you couldn't shake. You became lovers, tormentors, opponents, and in that time, you saw it all. Vacant-eyed bodies slumped in doorways, the black menace of cruising cars that transported drugs and death. No children resided here, only smaller weaker people who'd seen too much for a hundred lives. That was the life you shared with her—the street with no conscience and no compassion.

In twenty years, she hasn't changed. Tonight, you cruise your beat and feel the vibes that feed her. It's a certain rhythm all cops gauge as soon as they hit the street. As palpable as a pulse, it alerts your instincts and prepares you for the hours you'll spend together.

La Puta is quiet tonight. But that could change, *will* change, because this whore is deceptive. By now, you know her M.O. She lulls you into complacency, waiting to catch you unaware. Sometimes it's a gun that spits blue death, sometimes a glinting blade. The only thing certain is that she devours her victims like a frenzied animal circling fresh kill. Bloodlust that never ebbs, even after countless victims. Tonight, will you be hunter or hunted? There's never a clear answer, never only one, but that's part of the excitement, part of the game. What keeps you returning to this whore's embrace.

You troll the streets, past the liquor store where late night customers argue near the steel-barred doors. This evening's first on-view disturbance is a custody battle: two drunks fighting over a pint of cheap gin. Both are sufficiently juiced to present no real threat, but caution is the word tonight. La Puta throws curves sometimes. That gin bottle's a lethal weapon in the right hands, and you're not taking any chances. After relieving the combatants of their beverage of choice, you send them shambling on their way.

Ten minutes later, you notice the car that glides through a stop sign. Expired plates hang off the rusty bumper, and you hit your blue lights. Four blocks later, it still hasn't pulled over, in spite of your loud-speaker instructions. Six blocks, ten, and the car still proceeds at the stately pace of 10 miles per hour. The windows are dark enough to obscure the passengers. A cop-baiting ambush waiting to happen? You call in the plate number and request a back-up car.

"Got a chase?" asks the dispatcher.

"More like a procession. Less than 5 mph now, but the driver is weaving. Might be a set-up."

By the time your backup arrives, your nerves are humming. Finally, the car pulls over, and you both creep closer with weapons drawn. When the driver's door swings open, John Denver's reedy voice blasts out from the stereo in seismic waves that shake the hanging air freshener. A very pregnant lady is wedged behind the wheel, clutching a sticky spoon and offering you a sheepish, chocolate-rimmed smile. Balanced on her belly is a half-eaten quart of Fudge Ripple, some of which is dribbling down her chin. You can almost hear La Puta laughing.

The rest of the night uncoils like a languid snake. There's nothing major—burglar alarms, domestics, street disturbances that don't amount to much. An uneventful run of calls that would trick a less experienced man. But you can feel the momentum building amid this false calm—another of La Puta's games. For the thousandth time, you wonder how you can love a bitch who toys with you before she strikes.

It's nearly sunrise before she plays her final hand. Bands of color streak the sky, lighten the pall on the littered streets enough for you to spot the small figure standing near the alley. Smears of dirt and purple bruises cover what you guess to be a two-year-old face. His legs are bleeding from long strips of wounds, as though he was dragged through glass. Dressed in a filthy T-shirt and underpants, he watches you, unblinking. You've seen that look before— the fixed stare of the hopeless, the dull sheen of shock. Depthless eyes that don't respond even when you gather him in your arms. But as you cradle him, you see the other body that's crumpled against the wall.

You know without asking that this was his mother. Her eyes are glazed, her mouth lax and a paper bag clutched in rigid blue fingers. Nearby is the toluene can—the price of admission for her last final ride. Holding the shivering child, you can almost hear La Puta laughing. But there it is again, a thin mewling wail that comes from the dumpster. Praying and cursing, you find the boy's sister, a baby half-buried in the steeping trash. She's only days old and bluish, but her face is contorted, working on rage. A good sign for this new little life struggling to win her first battle with La Puta.

Her thready pulse tells you there's not much time. You take both babies back to your car, warming them as you radio for help. And then you wait, wondering if the sirens shrieking their approach are the ambulance, or La Puta conceding tonight's defeat.

Lip Lock

Another sticky summer night in Chicago. Even with the full moon rising, temperatures hover in the 90's—a guarantee that, on rookie cop Dennis Banahan's beat, it's going to be a busy night. Just a few months on the job has taught him that tempers flare and crime rises in direct proportion to the temperature. Since his assignment to the notorious 'Deuce,' Chicago's Second Police District, Dennis has worked the projects beat, a stretch of high-rise buildings called the Robert Taylor Homes. Shabby monoliths scarred by graffiti and the soot of frequent fires, they're the South side public housing equivalent of Cabrini Green. Each building is fifteen floors of gangs, drugs and attitude. Each night patrolling them is an adventure in staying alert and staying alive. In these quarters, rookie cops are forced to learn the job fast, to develop street instincts to ensure their survival. In the projects, there is no margin for error.

It's just past midnight, and Dennis and his partner are rolling out of the station lot. Tony's the wheel man tonight, and as usual they cruise down 40th Street to Federal, checking out the perimeter of their beat. The projects come alive at night. Sounds and smells assault the senses—distant screams, ripe garbage, burned rubber from squealing tires. Shots fired (or a car backfiring?), music pulsing—it all ebbs and flows in the night air. Like a pulse check, the two young cops gauge the rhythm of the streets—noting the bodies that slump in the doorways, the ones that retreat in the shadows. Down Federal Street to 44th, a left turn, and then another slow crawl up State Street.

It's when they're stopped at a light that they notice him. A little more than a block away, the man is standing in the street, slouched against a parked Oldsmobile. Early 20s, Dennis figures, maybe 6'2", 215 pounds. No gang colors, no baseball cap tipped to a certain angle. And, judging by his demeanor, nothing better to do than hang out in the street after midnight.

"Check out this guy," Dennis says. "Just standing there like he's waiting for a bus or something. Except the bus doesn't stop at Oldsmobiles."

"He's lookin' right at us," Tony notes. "Would've broke and run already if he was up to anything. Either he's high, or just some mope."

When the light changes, they drive slowly toward Mopey, finally pulling up along side him. Still slouched against the car, he doesn't move a muscle...except to pucker his lips.

"The guy's throwin' you a kiss!" Tony says. "Must like the way you look, Den. Maybe it's the blond hair."

"Fuck you! You're closer. It's you he wants to kiss!"

Puzzled, both cops stare at the man, who continues to pucker. Finally, Tony drives on.

"Screw this!" he snorts. "We stay any longer, the guy'll try to get lucky. This ain't my week for men!" But he turns at the next corner and circles the block. Another drive past Mopey, another offered kiss. Both cops know there's something hinky about this guy. The citizens in these parts throw a lot of things at uniformed cops, but it's *never* kisses.

The squad car glides away. This time, Tony approaches from a different angle, coming up a side street so they can view the other side of the Olds...and the other young man who's squatting behind it, stealing the tires.

In a flash, the rookies are out of the squad. Dennis grabs the thief, also known as Tyrone Dawkins, while Tony collars Mopey. As the handcuffs click into place, Tyrone glares at Mopey.

"Muthafucka, I *told* you to whistle if you saw the police!"

"And, muthafucka, I told *you* I don't know how to whistle!"

Dog Day

It wasn't that they were resistant to change. Just that, for the people who worked the early cars of the midnight watch, roll call was a sacred time. They had a standard routine that required no modifications. Depending on how their day had been spent—in court, under the covers, or catching up on chores at home—these first-watch cops slumped or lounging around the squad room knew one thing. Roll-call meant the final twenty minutes to wake up or nod off. Either way, being conscious wasn't usually required. Most nights, the field sergeant who held roll call simply counted bodies, called out beat assignments and mentioned anything noteworthy that occurred on the previous watch. That was the usual routine. But tonight, the regular field sergeant was on furlough and the usual routine was shot to hell.

"Teeeeeeeen-*HUT!*" At precisely 2245 hours, the booming command ricocheted through the room.

Slouched in the last row of seats, regular partners Moss and Zeller didn't budge.

"What the fuck?" mumbled Zeller without bothering

to open his eyes. "Some asshole recruit playin' soldier?"

Tipping his hat lower over his face, Moss only grunted. Damn shame when you couldn't get a few minutes sleep in your own squad room.

"I *said, FALL IN! Get off your asses and on your feet!*" This time, the voice registered on the Richter scale, a rumble loud enough to wake the dead. Which meant at least a half dozen of the twenty assembled officers opened their eyes. Before them stood a bulldog of a man, squat and barrel-chested, with lieutenant's bars glinting on his spotless white uniform shirt. And this particular bulldog was snarling—the Police version of James Cagney with an attitude. Reluctantly the watch shambled to their feet, straggled into a haphazard line.

"What is this, F-Troop? Show some pride, for Chrissake!" the Bulldog growled. "Look sharp, be sharp, that's my motto."

Near the end of the line, Moss rolled his eyes. "Gotta be a jarhead!" he whispered to Zeller. "Bet the next words out of his mouth will be 'semper fuckin' fi!'"

But the Bulldog was busy inspecting the troops, barking out questions as he went down the line.

"Where's your tie?"

"You call that a shoe-shine?"

"Where's your baton, Officer?"

"Don't those cuffs belong in a regulation case?"

By the time he got to Zeller, his face was studded

with sweat.

"What do you think, Officer?"

Zeller said nothing. It must be a trick question, he figured, and, when in doubt, the thousand-yard stare worked just fine.

"I *said,* what do you think about this? How do you expect to command respect as the Police when you look like a bunch of bums?"

"Don't matter what we look like, Lieutenant. This is a projects district. Nobody respects us here anyway." Zeller tried a smile—Christ, was this guy humorless?—but the Bulldog didn't blink.

"That's where you're wrong, son. You command respect by your demeanor and appearance. First thing we learned in the Marines." His gaze shifted to Moss, who was trying hard not to smirk.

"You were right. I *am* a fucking jarhead and proud of it." With a meaty paw, he thumped his chest. "No such thing as an ex-Marine. Semper fi." He waited, daring anyone to laugh. "Alright then. Take your seats, and let's get down to business."

His name, he said, was Less, Lieutenant Richard Q. Just beginning a 90-day assignment, detailed in from Headquarters. While he droned through a list of career credentials, everyone exchanged glances.

"His name's Dickless!" Moss whispered. "That figures. A desk jockey who probably ain't seen the streets for twenty years."

"No wonder his uniform's so clean," Zeller returned. "So much glare coming off that shirt my eyes are watering."

"...and unlike most supervisors, I prefer to be in the field with my troops," the Bulldog concluded. "So tonight I'll be out there with you. Monitoring your calls, going in on some of your jobs. Just to let you know I'm with you. Strength in numbers, men."

Moss and Zeller groaned in tandem. First their sleep was interrupted and now this, some dickless desk jockey playing John Wayne at Guadalcanal. Could it get any worse?

"Gonna be a long night," Zeller grumbled as they straggled out the door.

"Night?" Moss corrected. "Gonna be a long three months!"

Once in the privacy of their own squad car, though, the partners decided it might not be so bad. This was Friday, always a busy night in their West side district. Lt. Dickless would probably take a couple spins around the perimeter and call it a night—especially when he saw that these were the trenches out here. No poster cops in pristine uniforms worked this district. An hour, tops, Zeller figured, and the Bulldog would haul his pretty uniform right back into the station.

But Lt. Dickless wanted to see it all. Riding on the paddy wagon's "man down" call at Grenshaw and

Keeler, he was waiting at the scene when the wagon men pulled up.

"Nothing to get excited about, Boss," said Griffin, the senior partner. "Just a drunk passed out in the doorway."

"He could be armed. You should have your weapons drawn."

"Only weapon this guy's got is his breath." Rolling the inert man over, Silvestri tried not to laugh.

The Bulldog's next call was an assist for the Fire Department, given to Dante and Calhoun on Beat 1134. Pulling up to the corner of Wilcox and Campbell, the Lieutenant squinted at the 15-floor project building. Acrid smoke billowed from one of the top floor windows. Watching the firefighters unload coils of hose and equipment, he asked Calhoun about the procedure.

"Procedure?" Calhoun stared at him. "They go up there, they put out the fire. That's the procedure. And we go with 'em."

"To take the report," the Bulldog nodded. Paperwork was something he understood.

"To *protect* them. This is the projects, Lieutenant. And these guys are unarmed." Calhoun arched a brow. "You comin' with us, boss? It's on the fifteenth floor. Gotta take the stairs, though. Not a good idea to take the elevator."

"Looks like you have this under control," the

Bulldog blustered. "I'll just carry on."

Watching him drive off, Dante laughed.

"Probably didn't wanna mess up his clothes," he told his partner. "Soot stains are a bitch to get out."

For the next hour, the radio crackled relentlessly with urgent job assignments.

Man with a gun, gang fight on the street, battery in progress. At each scene, the Bulldog would roll up, get out and talk to the beat cops. No other action involved, no back-up or assistance, just a fleeting presence that came and went.

"What's the point of him being out here?" Moss asked Zeller. "Ain't like he's doing anything useful. Wandering around like some friggin' zombie."

"He's a boss. They all look like that." Zeller chewed his toothpick thoughtfully.

"Maybe he's tryin' to get his chops back for working the street."

"Maybe. Or maybe he never had any. Talks a good game, but it's all bull, y'know? You see how he backed off from that last street disturbance? What the hell kind of Marine does that?"

But there wasn't time to think about it. With non-stop jobs, the whole watch was too busy to worry much about the Bulldog. So busy that nobody even noticed he'd stopped appearing at their jobs.

It was almost 0600, nearly the end of the watch, when the call came over the radio. The transmitting voice was calm, interspersed with bursts of static.

"Beat 1199, requesting an ambulance and a back-up unit, Jackson and Artesian."

"1199?" Zeller asked. "Ain't that—"

"Dickless," finished Moss. "And what the hell is he doing over there?"

The location given was a project address—a rough beat for a two-man car, suicide for a desk jockey riding alone. Within seconds, all available units were speeding to the scene.

"Must be lost. Why else would he be cruising the projects at dawn?" Zeller wondered. "He forget to leave a bread crumb trail back to the station?"

The first car on the scene was 1115, Howell and Armstrong. Squealing up behind the Bulldog's deserted squad, they leaped out, expecting the worst. He'd been shot, they figured, or beaten and robbed, his service revolver shoved up his—

"Over here, guys." The calm voice came from just inside the building entrance.

While other squads came swerving up, the two cops drew their weapons and made their approach.

It was a legend in the making, they'd agree later. In the weeks and months that followed, at watch parties or the endless debates in smoky cop bars, all those who answered Bulldog's call would replay that scene, recount the story in endless variations. But the bottom line was always the same.

They found him in the murky project lobby, squatting on the concrete steps. It was too dark, at first, to see the baby in his arms, the one he cradled against his blood-soaked chest. Nearby, a weeping woman clutched her toddler son. And just beyond them, a lifeless man sprawled on the lobby floor with a single entry wound in his chest.

"Jesus H. Christ! What happened, boss?"

"Would-be rapist," he said. "Let's get a female officer here to take this baby. The ambulance is for Mrs. Powers and her son. She's okay, just shaken up. Little guy bumped his head, I think, so he'll need to be checked at the hospital."

Like a gentle giant, he rocked the squalling infant.

"This little one's okay. Just got scared when she heard the noise."

"Some noise," Armstrong whistled. There was enough space in the dead man's chest to park a bus. The Bulldog must have used a cannon.

Their lieutenant wasn't big on details, it seemed, even after the paramedics took the baby and they saw the switchblade buried in his shoulder. The Bulldog simply shrugged. It was no big deal, he said. He could drive himself to the hospital.

It was three weeks before the injured Lieutenant Less, Richard Q., was released from the medical roll and returned to duty. Three weeks before he strode into the squad room for midnight roll call and inspection of his troops. And, at first glimpse of the assembled watch, only seconds before his eyes threatened to tear. Every man and woman stood at attention, each in an immaculate uniform of the day. A "uniform" they'd selected solely for the Lieutenant's return: U.S. Marine Corps tee shirts bearing the snarling mascot bull dog.

"Teeeeeeen-*HUT!*" Zeller shouted when the Bulldog entered the room.

Twenty hands snapped up in a perfect salute, twenty pairs of well-polished shoes clicked together. Nineteen pairs of eyes stared ahead in correct military demeanor except for Moss, who winked at the Lieutenant.

"You know what they say, Boss. Semper fuckin' fi."

The Victims

BY GINA GALLO

"...It's only the kids who can still make me cry. Something happens to anyone else out here, I don't bat an eye. Not that I'm not sorry about it - some of what we see on this job is worst than any nightmare. Just that I've seen so much for so long, there's no tears left anymore.

It's like being numb. We have to be...otherwise, we'd all eat our guns."

Chicago Police Officer - 23 year veteran
September 1, 1997

Heart of a Champion

Kenny Brooks is his name. You've seen him around before. Been to his house any number of times on domestics, usually after his father's tossed back a pint to take off the edge and lay on the attitude. After a few swallows, he's ready to go a few rounds with his wife, his son Kenny or whoever's closest. Mama's a fighter too, not shy about creasing heads with her iron skillet. Kenny's body bears the history of their frequent brawls—scars and stitches and countless broken bones when he didn't duck fast enough. A medical history that doesn't particularly concern his parents. Most weekends, one or the other of them is hauled away in handcuffs, screaming and cussing so much the lockup keeper calls them the "Babbling Brooks."

Not exactly the picture of family harmony, and not the best example for a young kid. But in that tough Uptown neighborhood where role models are in short supply, the Brooks family fits right in. On Kenny's block, kids are gang members before they're ten, arrest statistics by fourteen. For them, higher education means graduating from jacking cars to stripping them. Survival there depends on sticky fingers, fast feet, and mastering the art of the hustle. Like the whores and thieves who loiter along North Racine Avenue, these kids learn early how to read a mark, strike fast and hit the ground running.

Which makes a kid like Kenny all the more unusual. Although you couldn't prove it by his school grades, he's a bright kid, more interested in making something of himself than making someone else. While his friends' dreams feature pimp-mobiles and a string of whores, Kenny's take him airborne. He wants to soar like a bird, or in this case, a Bull. What could be better than to be a part of the NBA's arena of champions? A much better direction to take his fast feet and quick reflexes. With a lot of practice and hard work, he might just be the next Michael Jordan. It makes perfect sense to Kenny. He's strong, and from the looks of things, on his way to being tall and sinewy. Already he's got the most important quality of all—a deep and unshakable love of the game. At the age of twelve, he's dedicated his heart to hoops and all his energy to being like Mike.

While the other kids are trolling the streets, looking for the next purse to snatch or a drunk to roll, Kenny's at the community center gym practicing endless drills. That's where a slice of light has brightened his narrow world in the form of Dexter MacBride, former ABA point guard and current volunteer coach for the center's athletic program. A long stretch of tight muscle and tough attitude, Coach Mac has a weeping demon tattooed on his right bicep. A souvenir, he says, of his two-year stint in prison, and a reminder of what happens when you allow yourself to detour from your dream.

Every afternoon from 3:30 to 5, he puts the line of sweaty kids through their paces, exhausting drills that leave them limp. For Kenny, it's the only glimpse of Heaven in his daily Hell, and Coach Mac, his living god. The routine's the same each day. While the boys run through their agility drills, the flint-eyed Coach watches silently. It's only when he distributes the balls for shooting practice that he begins the daily lecture, one Kenny has learned by heart.

"If you wanna be a champion, you gotta have the heart. Having the heart means you focus. You work hard. You push yourself past your limits. You make no excuses. And you never, ever let anything make you lose sight of your dream. You can't be a champion if you got a needle stuck in your arm, or you run the streets, or you're sittin' in some jail cell."

Shouting like an Evangelist preacher, the Coach's voice careens off the gym walls, promising salvation of another sort. For Kenny, his words are gospel .If you work hard, you'll ascend to the heaven of the basketball elite. Anything is possible if you stay focused, stay clean.

It helps to remember that when real life intervenes at home. Each time he dodges his father's fists, Kenny reminds himself of his dream. And tells himself that no matter what names his parents call him or how much they beat him, he still has a champion's heart. Champions don't quit. Champions have heart, and beat the odds no matter what.

The daily sessions with Coach Mac are making him stronger. Kenny feels it each time he enters the gym—as though all his problems fall away, leaving the absolute calm of concentration. Whenever he steps up to the line, nothing exists but the waiting hoop. Whether driving the lane or leaping into a perfect lay-up, the boy's movements are fluid grace, something the ever-scowling Coach notes with interest. Kenny is becoming an instrument of the game.

He decides it's time to drive the kid harder. Talent like Kenny's is rare. The Coach knows he has the heart, and judging from the scars that stripe his body, he's tough enough to go the distance. But even with talent, focus can shift and dreams fade, just as his had. He knows the flip side of the glory dreams, learned firsthand what turns them into nightmares. Watching the boy nail a perfect three-pointer, he feels the familiar bitterness rising up, concentrates on choking it back. No sense living in the past. In Kenny, his new protege, there's something to look forward to.

So he doubles the daily workouts. There's more coordination drills, tougher team plays, brutal scrimmages that send the boys flying. Kenny hangs tough through it all. And stays behind, after the other kids have limped off complaining, to get in some practice on his own. He wants to push himself past every limit, just like the champions.

Late one Friday afternoon, long after the others have gone, Kenny is still in the gym working on his jump shots. Without the echoed shouts and screaming whistles of the usual practice, he can concentrate on his rhythm and timing. Except for the ball slapping against the gleaming hardwood floor, it's quiet, as hushed as a cathedral. A perfect calm that has him dreaming. Which is why, at first, he barely hears the voice behind him.

Spinning out of a textbook fade-away, Kenny nearly trips over Coach Mac. Steel-band arms steady him before he topples over. It's the first time he's ever seen the coach smile.

"You got some nice moves there, boy. Keep it up, you're gonna be something one day."

A compliment tossed out with casual gruffness, but to Kenny, it means the world. Coach Mac *never* praises, no matter how well they perform. The most anyone's gotten is a grudging, "..well, it wasn't *too* bad!"

"I been watching you." Absently toying with his whistle's braided rope, the Coach nods. "You play like you got some heart. That's what I like to see."

In the face of such lavish praise, the boy is completely tongue-tied.

"You think you got what it takes, son? The heart of a champion?"

Awkward now, Kenny simply nods. But the fire in his eyes is unmistakable, reveals the same hunger and need that drove Jordan, and Shaq and the great ones who came before them. The same hunger that Dexter MacBride felt once.

"I been noticing how you go up for that fade-away," he continues. "If you put a little lean on your right side, it'll give you more control. Like this."

In a flash the Coach is airborne, gliding toward the hoop. The dunk is flawless, a master's gift to his dazzled student.

"Wow! That was awesome, Coach!"

"That was *rusty!*" he laughs. "Been a long time for this old man."

"You still got the moves, though. Can you show me some more?"

A heartbeat pause—just long enough to glimpse his reflection in Kenny's hopeful eyes.

"Yeah, I got some moves I can show you. But it's getting late now. What d'ya say we hit the showers?"

Heading off to the locker room, their voices and

footsteps are swallowed in that cavernous gym. Quiet descends, broken only by one single, tortured scream.

When the Crime Lab's Evidence Techs are called to the scene, they're astonished at what they find. But even their dozens of crime-scene photos won't answer what all of us wonder: how the skinny kid accomplished such an act. Dexter MacBride is sprawled on his side, his snarling face still purple. Ligature marks from his whistle's braided rope indicate that his death was quick but painful. His underwear is bunched around his knees, smeared with the blood of his twelve-year old victim.

At the hospital, Kenny is silent. Stares mutely when the Homicide dicks praise him for his bravery, and assure him that he did the right thing. And then they hover outside his room, the cops and doctors who whisper words like *brutal assault* and *traumatic injuries*. He knows they're waiting. His *statement,* they said. But he has no words now—maybe not ever. He's trying to focus, has to hang tough—the only way to shield his broken champion's heart.

Hurt Me

This had to be his lucky day. Just half a glass of Chardonnay and already she was purring, tracing lush lips with what looked like a very talented tongue. In a bar where most women expected a vat of Chivas and the deed to the ranch before they'd even say hello, this one barely made the two-drink minimum. A class act, he figured, judging by the rocks that winked at her ears and wrist. Just enough sparkle to catch the eye, not enough to cheapen her heartbreaker face. Same deal with her dress. A brief drape of wine-colored silk spilled over her ripeness, as fluid as her incredible eyes. Cat's eyes that watched, unblinking, while he stared at legs that went on forever, leading straight to paradise and a price tag he knew would be out of his league.

Now she traced silver nails up his thigh, purring approval when he stiffened. She wasn't big on small talk, not there, or in the car on the way to her place. It was one of those exclusive joints, a high-end address with a canopied portico and fawning doorman. Inside, all the trappings of deep pockets and deeper indulgence—terrazzo floors, silk wall coverings and a swift, silent elevator that delivered them to the penthouse suite. Whatever she did, or was about to do, she did very well. But she hadn't mentioned money yet, not a word about love for sale, so maybe this really was his lucky day.

Inside, more of the classy elegance that separated whore from high priced call-girl. No cheap frills for this babe, not a single red light or smoked mirror in sight. Instead, there were acres of thick carpeting that indicated no serious traffic tread on these floors, and enough silk upholstery to rival an emperor's palace.

He followed her into the bedroom, wondering. Nothing in there but the essentials—a lake-sized bed and a couple lamps. One of those artsy painted decorative screens favored by the rich or pretentious. But still no mention of money, something the working girls brought up right away. And here she was pulling back the satin bedspread, switching on the bedside lamps.

"I want to see you," she whispered. Obviously, a woman of few words—something he could definitely get used to. But what came next? Should he take off his pants or take out his wallet? There had to be a price-tag attached to this classy package. Better to get business settled first while he had a clear head.

But now she was stroking him again, easing down his zipper. Gently, she pushed him back on the bed, crawling toward him like a hungry cat. After that, he couldn't think at all.

There were flashes of light, swirling shadows, hot sweat and hammering blood. He was in heaven, or maybe hell, scorched by the fire of this beautiful demon. It didn't matter—*nothing* mattered as long as she didn't stop.

He wasn't sure when the rest started. Sometime after the feeding frenzy, after he'd spasmed his way into blissful exhaustion, she brought out her toys. A kinky cat, he realized, feeling himself harden again. And smiled when she rubbed against him, inviting him to play.

First, the scarves. Lengths of silk as slippery as her damp skin were wrapped around his wrists and legs. She kissed each knot that she tugged into place, nibbled his neck before slipping on the collar. And straddled him again, gripping his hair while she swallowed his moans.

"Do you want me to hurt you?" she asked.

"What?" He thrust against her, groaning. If this was hurt, bring on the pain.

Her wide cat's eyes glinted above him.

"Do you want me to hurt you? Tell me. You have to say it." Something was dragged across his chest, soft as a whisper. Smiling, she held it up for his inspection, a tiny flogger made of thin suede strips.

"Yes," he nodded. "Hurt me."

He'd never been more aroused. Naked and sleek, she flayed him softly, alternating the flogger's soft kisses with her own. And when a riding crop's sharper bite replaced the suede, it was ecstasy that had him moaning, exquisite pleasure-pain in every blow.

"Say it!" she commanded. This time, a narrow leather strap licked his thighs.

"Hurt me!" The pain grew sharper, as strong as her scent filling his head. She was everywhere, stroking and biting while she reached for another strap. Handcuffs snapped into place but he barely noticed, not while she licked his welted skin, traded drugging kisses for numbing pain. He couldn't think, didn't know what was happening, or what was real.

"Again," she whispered, licking his ear. "Say it."

"Stop," he groaned. "No more."

"Just one more time, and I'll stop. I promise."

"...hurt me."

But she didn't move. Those cat's eyes glowed golden now, almost shimmering in the light. Beautiful, he thought, how the light dappled her body. A perfect goddess who knelt above him, smiling. Another kiss—sweet this time, and softer.

"Game's over?" he asked.

"You can relax now. It's over," she said. And waited for his eyes to drift closed before she reached for the knife.

Afterward, they decided it was one of their best. Sure to be one of the biggest sellers, she told the camera man concealed behind the screen. Popping out the video tape, he agreed. This one had it all. The screams and moans, the beating, and a vivid death sure to satisfy their most discerning customers. Took the poor guy a long time to die, but every bit of it was captured on tape. Not every snuff film maker paid such attention to detail.

Rites of Spring

It happens every year. For a snowbelt city like Chicago that forfeits three to five months of each year to ice, blizzards and freezing temps, the warm weather that heralds Spring's arrival brings certain rituals that are strictly observed. Rituals that vary depending on which city neighborhood is involved. As the mercury rises, the North side's Gold Coast residents leave the gilt-edged wombs of their high-rise penthouses for a refreshing stroll down Michigan Avenue. Inhabitants of the South side Bridgeport neighborhood watch cleaning crews spruce up Comiskey Park for the White Sox' Opening Day festivities. And city dwellers everywhere jog along the 70-odd miles of Lake Michigan's beaches, anticipating the warmer days to come.

But for residents of Keisha Samuels' South side neighborhood, there are no lakeside sprints or promenades down the Magnificent Mile. Englewood is the formal name for this particular pocket of Hell—an area populated by more gangs than anywhere else in the city. Violent crimes are commonplace in these parts—drive-bys, homicides, rapes and robberies—such large numbers they seldom make the newspapers. Another stabbing in "the 'Wood?" What else is new? Another women raped at the El station? Maybe she should move to another neighborhood. The Crime Index rises along with the temperature and, come Spring, the hustlers and gangsters hit the street with a vengeance, ready for another long hot season.

Just ten years old, Keisha Samuels has seen it all. She already knows the tacit laws of her neighborhood, is well acquainted with the way street gangs gear up for their own Spring rituals. Warm weather means the 'bangers will hit the streets, intent on establishing their rank in the gang power hierarchy. On this brutal landscape, there are few spring gardens, few tender blossoms to mark the changing season. Instead, it's blood and carnage that color these streets where warring gangs jockey for position. Gang turf is acknowledged, challenged, divided according to numbers: whoever has the most guns, the most members, the most force. Opening season in the 'Wood means the first drive-by shootings, the first blood spilled to send a clear message: Dominance or death.

Like other Englewood kids, Keisha's childhood illusions were as short-lived as the junkies nodding in the gutter. Raised in this inferno with screaming sirens for lullabies, babies grow up—and old, quickly.

In Englewood, hopscotch is played on blood-smeared sidewalks, corpses discarded in dumpsters along with the trash. A street-smart kid like Keisha knows that the elements for survival are equal parts awareness and luck, keeping your eyes open and your mouth shut. Experience brings harsh lessons, and already she's had her share. Just last year her brother Anthony was killed, another victim of Englewood's gangs. And her father—that man in the picture Mama keeps in a big silver frame—was a gang member himself, gunned down before he was twenty. Before Keisha was even born.

Now she's the oldest child, the designated protector of four younger kids. While Mama works, it's Keisha who's the parent, Keisha who guards the family home. And, with the advent of Spring, it's Keisha who decides to observe a ritual of her own. Springtime means the season opening of Fat Johnnie's Hot Dog Stand, a venerated Chicago land-mark on south Western Avenue. Started as a simple street stand more than 30 years before, Fat Johnnie's gained infamy for the quality and variety of its trade-mark "Chicago dogs"—over 50 variations that brought the attention of the media, culinary magazines and a huge following of hot dog gourmands from all over the city. Cited by Chicago newspapers as "the dog you LOVE to bite," a Fat Johnnie's hot dog is Keisha's favorite rite of Spring. And when the boards are removed on opening day, she's there, standing in a line that curls around the block.

Her brothers and sister are left at home to wait for the goodies. She knows better than to bring them along. Western Avenue is a busy thoroughfare with heavy truck traffic, and a phalanx of gang members lounging on the corners, armed and ready for potential intruders. A dangerous street to negotiate with a pack of squalling kids. Easier to make the trip alone.

Finally, Keisha steps up to the counter and places her order. One chili-cheese dog for her, heavy on the relish. Super-dogs for Malik and Troy, hold the hot peppers. Rochelle wants a "mother-in-law": a tamale tucked into a poppy seed bun, smothered with chili. And for five-year-old Quincy, a double dog with the works: tomato, mustard, onion, relish, pepper, cucumber strip, celery salt and pickles. Lots of pickles.

The food smells like ambrosia. Scents so tantalizing, Keisha is tempted to rip into the bag as soon as it's placed in her hands. Nothing tastes better than the season's first hot dog on a warm Spring day, but the kids are waiting at home. Just four blocks to go, and they can all enjoy them. Four blocks through the war zone of Englewood.

Clutching her bag tighter, Keisha reads the street. Gangster Disciples on the first corner, caps tilted to the left, are flipping gang signs at passing cars. By cutting through the alley to 73rd street, she can avoid them and make it across Western. Which still leaves the drug dealers on Claremont to get past, and the Imperial Gangsters hanging out on Oakley Avenue. She starts down the alley. Runs an extra block out of her way when she spots the low-rider, a blue Pontiac with blacked-out windows that creeps down the street. Blue is the color of rival gangs in this part of Englewood, and she's not taking chances.

By cutting through some hedges and across an empty lot, she avoids the two men arguing over a dime bag on Bell Avenue. She ducks down another alley. Nearly home now. She slows to a walk, as much to catch her breath as to imagine that first bite of hot dog, the delight of her brothers and sister. The "big sister" thrill of introducing them to this particular rite of Spring. And is just approaching Hamilton Avenue when she hears it—the shriek of tires swerving around the corner. The Pontiac again, this time with windows lowered just enough to steady the gun muzzles aimed at the street.

Survival mode kicks in. Still clutching her bag of food, Keisha races down the street, vaulting over bushes, ducking between buildings. A volley of shots rip through the air, followed by tortured screams. She never looks back. Legs pumping furiously, she cuts between the parked cars for the final sprint to her house. The kids are watching from the window. Keisha can see them all—even Quincy's beaming grin when he spots the bag she carries. But she never sees the Nissan sedan coming toward her, flashing silver in the sun.

Later, the Nissan's driver will explain to the police that he never saw the little girl. That she rushed into the street before he could stop. And he'll weep without consolation as he watches the paramedics' blanket settles in damp red patches over Keisha's body...and hears the officer's dire words.

"It happens every Spring."

12 Sq. Ft., River View

It used to be a swamp. Years ago, before the settlers came, and the opportunists who reinvented Chicago as an architectural wonderland, there was nothing here but swamp, marshy grasses, and the stench of wild onions, which flourished along Lake Michigan. The smell was so disturbing and pervasive it prompted the Indians to name the area: Chee-caw-gah, literally translated as *bad smell*.

Time and money changed Chicago's landscape. The muddy frontier settlement was transformed by funds from the meat-packing czars,and other titans of industry who made fortunes in this city beyond their wildest dreams. What once was swampland became the glittering "Second City." Clever architects designed what would become breathtaking skyscrapers along the shoreline. Lakefront properties that sold for a king's ransom became affluent enclaves with names like "the Gold Coast" and "River North," inhabited by moneyed glitterati who understood the most important principle of real estate: location is everything.

There are still some areas of Chicago that suggest

its humble beginnings. Lower Wacker Drive is one of these. It's a thoroughfare that runs beneath the downtown Loop streets, a virtual labyrinth of tunnels level with the Chicago River. For anyone who knows how to navigate through the confusing maze, it's an easy shortcut to avoid heavy Loop traffic.

In these nether tunnels exists a community that isn't mentioned in the real estate guides, and is never included in tourist itineraries. It's the City of Boxes, where throngs of homeless people huddle together, residing in crates and packing cartons discarded by the delivery trucks that rumble through Lower Wacker.

Survival in these quarters is a tricky thing. Like real estate everywhere, location is important. For those persons lucky enough to position their boxes nearest the garbage bins of the restaurants above, a foraged meal is usually guaranteed. When winter comes, a spot close to heat conduits provides some relief from the bitter elements. But there's never respite from the predatory rats with a taste for human flesh, or the drunks and thieves who would—and do—kill for the last swallow of rot-gut wine.

Lottie Maynard knows all this. She's a veteran of the survival game, homeless for nine years, or, as the social workers say, "indigent." At forty-six years of age, she looks seventy, feels even older. Her body bears the transcript of her street education: fibrous scars from previous stabbings, a dragging limp, and, courtesy of a former pimp's vicious beating, punctured eardrums. A survivor, but barely, in a world where the crippled and weak are carrion.

Which is why Lottie is careful to be invisible. While most of the box people huddle near the building walls, or beneath the loading docks, Lottie resides in a packing crate near the river. It's colder here, with a sharp wind that carries the stench of garbage, but at least she's alone, away from the predators. Her crate is tucked away behind a dumpster, undetectable from the access road that borders the water. She considers herself lucky. In the netherworld of street real estate, hers is a prime location. At night, the river glints like fluid glass as she contemplates the spectacular skyline view. A parade of bleating tugboats pass her each morning, heralding another day of staying alive.

On the street each day, Lottie makes her rounds. Panhandling comes first, enough to buy a bracing pint of whiskey. Food later, if she can beat the rats to the dumpsters. If not, there's always the Mission shelter, a place she'd rather avoid. Not because of the pre-meal de-lousing shower, or even the religious sermon afterward. That's fair trade, she figures, for a hot meal and a few hours out of the cold. But the shelter is full of street people she likens to wild dogs, with pack behavior that dictates survival of the fittest, the meanest, the cruelest. People who could hurt or destroy a weaker, crippled woman.

So Lottie remains invisible, only venturing down deserted alleys, fading into the shadows when night falls. Then she retreats to the security of her crate, twelve square feet that's both home and sanctuary. Away from the others, without friends or acquaintances, hers is a silent, ordered existence that trades loneliness for safety.

Sometimes, on nights like this when the cold seeps in, bringing wind as relentless as her wheezing cough, she hugs herself, remembering.

There was another life once, another time when she was young and free, her body an asset instead of a curse. When people could see her, smile at her, watch the way her hips moved as she sauntered down the street. When she could still hear their voices, the humming approval of men with hungry eyes and fevered hands. Now she's invisible, and hears nothing but the bleak monotone of her silent world.

A car swerving down the access road brings Lottie out of her reverie. Automatically she curls herself tighter, retreats farther into her crate. It's a red car, a rusty old Pontiac coming closer, down the embankment, toward the clumps of bushes. Lottie frowns, wondering. There's no reason to come here, nothing around but garbage and weeds. And no one ever comes down that road, not at night, and never by car. It's not even a road, really, just a rocky dirt path barely wide enough for one person. Shivering in her secret den, Lottie watches.

Less than ten feet away, the car stops. Two men get out, one taller than the other. They're so close, she can see their faces as they help—or pull—a third person from the back seat. It's a young girl—small, slender and terrified as the leering men circle her.

She can't hear their voices, but Lottie knows that look. She's seen it before, the bloodlust of predators about to devour their kill. The taste of fear sours her mouth, keeps her a silent witness. There's nothing she can do, no way she can prevent what's about to happen. Choking back the nausea, she watches, and remembers.

The girl is crying now. Blood trickles from her lips, tears leak out of eyes already swelling from the blows. In futile defense, her arms fly up, crossing her narrow chest as she cowers. Fueled by her fear and her submission, the men laugh. Her clothes are torn, tossed aside to reveal more bruises. So young, Lottie thinks, hardly more than a child. A fragile island in a world of trouble.

The vicious scenario plays out like a savage, silent movie. No screams or moans invade Lottie's sound-less world, only frightening grisly freeze-frames. She doesn't want to watch it, can't pull her eyes away from the rutting animals or their helpless prey.

It becomes an awful game. The men take turns, first one, then the other, grunting and sweating, offering each other their bleeding bounty. And when it's over, it still isn't enough. Panting, struggling to adjust his own clothes, one man watches while the other raises his hand, and what looks like a club, for the final round. That club descends, again and again, until the game is over and the winners move on.

The dark dissolves to pallid dawn before Lottie dares to move. A secret sentry, she mourned through the night while the girl's fluids bubbled hot and thick over the frozen ground, waited for her twitching limbs to finally still. Now the body is a silent reproach. Like a broken toy, Lottie thinks. The girl was too young to know about being invisible. It was the only thing that might have saved her.

It's almost light now, nearly time for Lottie to start her rounds. But she can't leave this little girl. Something should be done, she thinks mournfully. Not that anything can help her now.

Stiffly, Lottie shambles forward in her crate. Closer to the body, close enough to see a dusting of freckles on the bluish skin. Pulling her ragged coat tighter, she shivers in the brittle cold. And wonders if there's a family somewhere waiting for this child, a mother praying for her missing daughter.

Tears fall unheeded, become heaving sobs. Fisting her hands at streaming eyes, Lottie drops to the ground, keening over the body. She should have stopped it, wanted to do something but—what? What can you do when you're invisible?

Still kneeling, Lottie's lips move in prayer, barely remembered from her other life. A eulogy or confession of her own sin?

"...forgive us our trespasses, as we forgive those who trespass against us..."

Her voice trips over the arcane language of the ancient prayer. Tentatively, she reaches out, strokes the chilled skin—and feels it. A pulse, barely detectable, bumps against her fingertip. Startled, she pulls her hand back. It can't be possible. Not now, not after...everything. But her hand reaches out again, searching. There. Faint as a whisper, thready, but there.

The prayer is forgotten. Awkwardly, Lottie gathers the body in her shaking arms. It's not too late. She can help her now, save this child she couldn't protect. Choking back a sob, she struggles to lift the frail girl. Too heavy, in spite of her slight frame, so Lottie drags her back to the refuge of her crate. They'll be safe here, invisible. Lottie's thoughts race. There's a blanket here to warm her. And food—still some left from last night's foraging. Later, she'll find a way to care for her wounds. The girl is alive, and everything will be fine.

She tucks her tattered blanket around the girl. Next

comes her threadbare coat, and finally the sweater—
whatever will keep her warm. Although she shivers,
Lottie doesn't notice the cold, or even the way her
home is tilting at an odd angle. In her silent world
she's oblivious to the sounds of whirring machinery.
And those vibrations? It must be the beating of her
own heart. Exertion and fear can do that. But it's
over now. Thank God it's over, and the girl is still
alive. Lottie murmurs yet another prayer—one of
thanksgiving this time. After a few decades of absti-
nence, praying requires concentration, so she closes
her eyes...and thinks about life and death and second
chances. And never sees the huge steel jaws of the
sanitation truck that rip through her home, devouring
the crate, the broken child and the invisible woman.

Mouths of Babes

It's the usual curriculum. For kindergarten classes in Chicago's Public School system, the basics are taught—the ABC's, Coloring 101, Number recognition and, to help the kiddies develop some social skills, Intro Playground. For some kids, it's enough. For others, like Miguel Ramos, it's nothing.

He's a difficult case, the teachers agree. They've seen his kind before—the dysfunctional child of a child. His mother's just seventeen and seems...well, irresponsible. And the father? They've never seen Miguel's father—not even sure he's around, so that can't bode well. Since Spanish is the language spoken at home, Miguel doesn't understand much English. Hard to tell *what* he understands since he doesn't speak, merely stares at his teachers with those big dark eyes that seem centuries older than his face. During class, he tracks the colored letters of the flashcards, the bright pictures of puppy and kitten and car, and shows no emotion, no recognition at all.

"Learning disability," his teachers murmur, and then shake their heads. In the overcrowded, under-staffed inner city schools, it's easy for a kid like

Miguel to fall through the cracks. But the teachers do what they can. Patiently line the crayons along the boy's desk, point out the colors, repeating numbers drawn on the board, and hope that something sinks in.

What they don't know is that Miguel is already a *cum laude* graduate of the School of Hard Knocks, a degree conferred to children in his circumstances. His daddy Javier's been in prison longer than Miguel's been alive. A narcotics bust sent him up, one he took the dive for, but that can happen when you're in a gang. Nobody rats on their brothers—it's part of the code of the street. So Raoul sits in a 6x8 cell at Stateville, marking time and wondering about the son he's never seen.

Miguel's mother? Already leeched of their childish roundness, Alicia's arms and face bear the tattoos that mark her as an Insane Cobra. The same gang her parents were in, the same that will embrace her son. Miguel is a gang baby—a cycle that starts at birth, ends when the casket is lowered into the ground. And in between, whatever fate allows.

For gang babies, even their christening is a pledge of allegiance. After the Church's standard religious ritual, gang members bring their baby home for a night of revelry. Like most other families, except that here the bassinette is draped in gang colors—Cobras' green and black for Miguel. No christening gown, only a tiny set of gang colors that herald the baby as a future 'banger. And photographs of the blessed event that show the proud parents, flashing gang signs in the background, pointing to the baby. His tiny hands are crossed over the black semi-automatic pistol they placed on his chest. A totem for the bloodshed to come, or an indication that this baby is already dead...it'll just take a few years for the bullet to catch up with him.

But Alicia doesn't think about that much. It's hard on the street without her man, harder still with a kid. Hard to scrape up the money for food and drugs and the party life she still desires. Cobras are expected to run with their set. She needs their friendship, and more than that, their protection. Gang women aren't safe alone out here, and without Javier, anything can happen. The other Cobras look out for her, but like everything else, protection costs. Her body is still the currency that pays the fee, but there are younger, finer bitches out there, threatening to replace her. Girls who don't live minute to minute worrying about the next fix. It's oblivion Alicia buys with a needle and a spoon, escape from the thrusting men who use her and move on. At seventeen, she's strung out, used up, and beyond caring about anything but getting high.

So when the phone calls come from Miguel's school, Alicia ignores them. The *gueras* are crazy— there's nothing wrong with her kid. He knows plenty!

At five years old, he already knows how to chamber a round in the family guns—an important lesson in the survival game. He knows about gang loyalty, and protecting what's his. How to identify friends and enemies. And didn't she teach him how to bag marijuana for street sales, adding enough stems to increase the gram weight? Her kid is smart—street smart. In the Cobras' world, that's all that matters.

When the phone calls give way to letters, she brushes them aside. Miguel doesn't have a learning disability! So what if he doesn't talk? Better that than to be jabbering and screeching like some little brats. She knows he's normal, even if she doesn't spend much time with him herself. Hanging out and getting high takes up a lot of her time, but Miguel can handle it. Teach him to be independent—a real man, just like his Daddy.

So Miguel's teachers do what they can. Flashcards and numbers and color names are patiently repeated to the silent staring boy. While the other children play in the schoolyard, he stands alone. No reaction moves his somber face, no emotion lights his ancient eyes.

But on one Friday morning, everything changes. Miguel's class is visited by "Officer Friendly," a cop who comes to speak with the kids. Taking in the blue uniform and silver badge, Miguel's eyes widen in recognition. He's seen cops before, all over his neighborhood, and hears his mother speak of them. And she spits afterward, like a curse.

But this cop is different. He's got a gun—another thing Miguel knows about, and he's smiling. He walks around the room, joking and laughing, showing pictures to the kids. Talking about some bad dude named "Stranger Danger." Miguel turns the unfamiliar words over in his mind. He mouths them silently, savoring the feel. "Stranger Danger." English words that mean trouble.

The class listens intently to Officer Friendly. The big cop shows other pictures—large drawings of the trouble Stranger Danger can bring. You never know where he'll turn up, the cop says. Could be on the street, or in a car. Miguel thinks of the drive-bys in his neighborhood and nods. He knows all about Stranger Danger. And figures that maybe this is one cop who's okay. He knows about taking care of business, protecting against enemies. Like the Cobras, Officer Friendly carries a gun, and he wears blue like the other cops, which must be the color of *his* gang. The little boy nods again. It's part of the street code, just like the Cobras. And for the first time, Miguel's teacher sees him smile.

Several nights later, police respond to a "shots fired in the house" call at Miguel's address. A man's bleeding body is sprawled across the threshold, and even in the dim light, his prison tattoos are clearly discernible. It's Javier, recently paroled and returning home to his wife and child. The wife who now nods incoherently over a crack pipe while the child holds a smoking 9mm Glock. Catching sight of the approaching police, Miguel points at his dying father, and proudly, carefully speaks those exotic English words:

"Stranger Danger."

Probable Cause

Summer in the city. It's one of the hottest in Chicago history, and a new record for July with eighteen straight days of searing temps that hover near the 100 degree mark. Even at midnight, the air is still heavy with the simmering heat. In Fillmore, the Eleventh Police District, roll call has ended and the first watch cars are rolling out of the station lot. Tonight, Frye and Padilla are partnered together, two young rookies with less than four years street experience between them.

As far as they're concerned, Fillmore is the best district for arrests, excitement and non-stop action. With its rampant gangs, assorted mopes and the high-rise projects called Rockwell Gardens, a single midnight tour in Fillmore can feel like a year behind the barbed wire of Sarejevo.

Both Frye and Padilla are conscientious cops who take their police duties seriously. Which means that at least two hours of their daily personal routine involves some heavy pumping at the gym, just to stay in fighting shape. Behind the wheel tonight, Padilla fidgets with his safety vest, which the relentless heat has fused to his back. Already his uniform is soaked with sweat.

"It's like a friggin' sauna out here," he grumbles to his partner.

"So hit the all-night car wash and drive through," Frye shrugs. "From the smell in here, this pig can use a good cleaning." He kicks aside the half-eaten rib-tips thoughtfully left by the previous beat cops—the most recent addition to the collection of fast food wrappers, coffee cups and assorted soda cans that litter the floor. "If we don't get some of this junk outta here, the rats are gonna commandeer this car at the first stop light."

"You kidding? No rat in his right mind would eat the crap that cops do. It's why they survive anything and we don't!"

Padilla considers the car wash idea. A refreshing drive-through, with the windows open, would be just the thing. Like taking a shower without the bother of getting undressed. In this heat, his uniform blues would dry within minutes. Before he can decide, the radio crackles to life.

"Attention all units in the Eleventh District, all units on citywide, we have an armed robbery that just occurred at the liquor store, 28— W. Madison. Repeat, an armed robbery just occurred, California and Madison at the liquor store. Offenders fled on foot southbound from that location..."

As the description of the offenders is broadcast, Padilla whips the car around.

It's tacit agreement between these two that they ride on any hot call. While Padilla floors the accelerator, Frye repeats the descriptions.

"Two male blacks, twenty to twenty-five years old. Number one's six foot, one-seventy, black tee shirt, dark jeans, cornrows..."

"That's half the male population in this district!" Padilla grunts.

"...Number two's five foot seven inches, hundred and fifty, white tee shirt, blue jeans, short fade haircut..."

"Oh, that narrows it down!"

"....southbound from that location. Number two was last seen running near Adams and Mozart. Nothing else on number one."

"We're two blocks from Mozart. Let's check it out."

With the kamikaze driving skills mastered by every street cop, Padilla swerves around corners, weaves through slower traffic and barrels under a viaduct.

"Over there!" Frye shouts. "Walking near the mail box. White shirt, blue jeans, short fade."

Padilla slams on the brakes, fishtailing to a stop. The subject in question stiffens—that deer-in-head-lights freeze that, in the ghetto, is preparatory to beating feet. This time is no exception. When Frye leaps out of the car, Mr. Short Fade hauls ass.

While Padilla follows in the car, Frye chases Fade

down Mozart, across Jackson, through gangways and under stairways. Since Fade is small, wiry, and dressed to run in gym shoes (called "felony flyers" by cops), he keeps a good distance from the young cop, who huffs along in high-top steel-toed boots, a Kevlar safety vest and a 30 pound gun belt. In this heat, any exertion is taxing. A long run while strapped into ghetto commando gear can be dangerous. Still, all those hours in the gym have paid off. Frye leaps over bushes, darts across empty lots as nimbly as his prey, and six blocks into the chase, isn't close to getting winded. What he is getting is pissed off.

Funny thing about a foot chase. At the beginning, the motivation is to get the bad guy because he did something wrong. A few blocks into it, your reasoning shifts. Now you want him because he had the nerve to run. Several blocks more, and you're really mad. You're starting to get side stitches, you have no idea where your partner is, you've lost at least ten pounds of sweat and you want to make this guy as miserable as you feel. Ninety friggin' degrees and he's running like a damned greyhound? He definitely needs to be caught!

By the time Frye races across his fifth empty lot, he's way beyond pissed. Huffing up a steep railroad embankment, he has no idea where Padilla is. It isn't his partner's fault. No way could he have followed them through backyards or under drainpipes. And

Frye doesn't exactly have the time to radio his location. Hell, he isn't even sure where he is now. Up on the tracks somewhere, and might end up in Cleveland before this fool stops running. If Frye doesn't have a heart attack first.

Finally it happens. Jumping over some railroad ties, Fade stumbles. The felony flyers slip in the gravel and he falls ass over teakettle down the embankment. It's all Frye needs. He vaults toward him in a classic linebacker tackle. Two hundred and forty pounds of cop and accessories knock the wind, the fight and the attitude out of Fade. Flat on his back, he coughs and chokes, raising one arm up in defense. After a two-mile all-terrain chase, Frye is in no mood for tender mercies. Heaving and gasping, he raises his fist.

"What. The. Fuck. Is. Wrong. With. You. Asshole?" A rhetorical question, punctuated by well-placed punches to make sure he gets his point across. Although he doesn't really expect an answer, Fade's passive gurgling enrages him. It's only after a few more minutes of serious ass-kicking that Frye realizes his captive has passed out, or possibly died. The moisture running down his face is not sweat, but blood splashing off his fists from Fade's mangled features. The smaller man's face is a mash of pulp and gore, streaming blood where teeth used to be.

Rocking back on his heels, Frye waits for his

breathing to steady. Only then does he hear the wail of sirens nearby. Finally, his back-up—after two or three miles and untold gallons of sweat. He swipes at his brow, considers his inert captive, and waits for the cavalry to arrive.

At Cook County Hospital, where Fade is transported via paddy wagon for emergency care, Frye learns that his prisoner will live, but barely. His skull is fractured, six ribs broken, and a lung punctured. And a mug so badly damaged, Padilla notes, that the guy could be eligible for a face donor.

It's then that the field sergeant arrives to give them the news. Both suspects of the armed robbery have been taken into custody.

"So where'd they find the other guy?" Padilla asks.

"Both guys," the sergeant corrects. "They got both of them, and the weapons, about twenty minutes ago. The liquor store owner made a positive I.D. on both of them."

Padilla and Frye can only stare.

"Both guys? Then who's this mope?"

"You tell me. And considering he's half dead, it better be something good."

"Oh, man!" *Oh shit!*

It isn't until hours later, when Fade has regained consciousness and is able to wheeze out a few words that the cops get the whole story. Their "prisoner" is identified as Jerome Beauregard, employed as a maintenance man at the Way of the Divine Light Missionary Baptist Church. Jerome had just finished cleaning up after a youth ministry meeting and was on his way home when the cops saw him.

The nurse who hovers at Jerome's bedside can barely keep her lip from curling. Her eyes shoot daggers at the young cops. They can hear what she's thinking—*police brutality,*—as clearly as the hissing oxygen.

Frye lowers his head close to Jerome.

"Man, if you didn't do anything, then why the hell did you run?"

The mangled lips barely move behind the oxygen mask.

"Because you was chasin' me."

The
Crimes

"...why you frontin' me like I'm some kind of monster, dude? Seems to me like you and me, we in the same business. Only thing is, I get locked up for it, and you get a paycheck and a pension."

Homicide offender to the arresting officer
November 26, 1989

Penalty for
Early Withdrawal

"Fast, friendly service from folks who care. The neighborhood bank for all your financial needs."

That's the slogan of the Southlawn Bank. A small building nestled between a dry cleaner's shop and Gus and Nick's Gyros Supreme, the bank has served Chicago's south side working class community for over seventy years. It's not a fancy place. As the bank president explains, their services are geared toward the blue collar community—the average working stiff trying to get a down payment for one of the small brick bungalows that line the neighborhood streets. Since a more sophisticated financial institution might be intimidating to this community, Southlawn keeps it simple—friendly service and a helpful staff—the winning combo that keeps their customers coming back.

Which may be why Alonzo Weeks chose Southlawn to handle his particular financial needs. Striding into the small lobby that July morning, he marched up to the teller's window and announced that he wanted to open a savings account. Clarice Osinski smiled vaguely. Her hair was cut short enough to display pearl earrings and a sizable hearing aid. Noticing it, Alonzo repeated his question louder, then flipped his wallet open to display the bills inside—one hundred in all—just to give her a visual aid.

"Have a seat at that first desk," Clarice told him. "Our accounts representative will be with you in a moment."

While Alonzo waited, he checked out the friendly bank. The two tellers—Clarice and another lady—did indeed seem friendly, and not much of a threat. An older woman with drooping jowls and thick bifocals was parked behind the information desk. The sign next to her invited customers to ask about Southlawn's Christmas Club. No threat there either. Glancing out the window, he saw the green Mercury idling at the curb. That was Odell, his wheel man, waiting as planned. Perfect.

Alonzo sized up the bank's interior. A youngish typist at the next desk was busy yakking on the phone, oblivious to anyone. Behind the tellers' windows were two security cameras—not exactly state-of-the-art, as far as he could see. Neither camera pivoted—hell, they probably couldn't even focus through the thick layers of dust coating the lenses. And some skinny kid with bad skin and a starter mustache was lounging just outside in a doorman's uniform, nodding in the morning light. As far as protective measures went, the friendly bank was still in the Dark Ages. Alonzo had come to the right place.

When the new accounts representative bounced up and introduced herself, Alonzo's answering smile was sincere. Tiffany Knowles looked barely out of high school. The fluorescent light glinted off her braces as she offered a freckled hand. This was going to be easier than he thought.

"A savings account," he told her, placing his wallet on the desk.

Alonzo's hand slipped under his shirt for the revolver in his waistband—or where it had been before it slipped down. From the feel of things, it was now nestled somewhere lower, pinching him right through his boxers. Slumping lower in his chair, Alonzo tried to dig it out without being conspicuous. Not an easy thing to do since the damned gun was caught in his fly.

"I really appreciate your help," he said to Tiffany, who watched him curiously. "And I think you're very nice, so please don't take this personally."

Wincing just a little because the trigger guard was caught in some hair, he leaned closer and whispered, "I'm holding you up."

Tiffany's polite smile was automatic, the product of

her friendly employee training.

"Oh, no, sir. Take your time. I have all the time in the world."

"No. That ain't what I mean." He tugged again—on his testicles this time—which seemed to be skewered by the gun muzzle. Should have brought a snub-nose instead of the .38. The last time he'd take Odell's advice about anything! Another tug, and he felt his skin tear. Alonzo couldn't suppress the moan.

By now the typist had turned to stare. Swiveling, she watched wide-eyed as the guy in the flowered shirt fumbled around in his crotch. What kind of weirdo was *this?* His eyes were glassy and he was starting to sweat—the classic signs of a sex pervert.

"Look out, Tiffany, this guy's gonna flash his dick!" she screeched. Even for the Southlawn Bank, that was taking friendly too far. Picking up the closest weapon—a plastic bud vase with one shriveled carnation, she lobbed it in Alonzo's direction. It bounced off his shoulder and rolled across the rug.

"You bitch!" Alonzo screamed, leaping up. "This is a *hold-up,* fer Chrissakes!" His hands groped frantically for his weapon, now hopelessly caught in pubic hair and fabric.

"I got a goddamn *gun!* Just give me all your money so I won't have to kill anybody!" Which might have been a considerable threat if his pants hadn't started to fall. The back end of his khakis and boxers slipped down together so far he inadvertently mooned the information lady.

"No coins!" he growled to the astonished Tiffany. "Put all the paper money in a brown bag or you die! Do it now!"

At the teller's window, Clarice was craning her neck. All they usually got was deposits and withdrawals, but this morning it was a whole floor show. The bare-assed customer in the middle of the lobby was doubled over with both hands at his groin. Maybe it was cramps.

Tiffany was perplexed. This guy didn't look like a robber, but then she'd never seen one before. On the other hand, she was pretty sure bank robbers didn't usually drop their drawers in the middle of the lobby. The whole thing was strange—especially since he wouldn't stop howling.

Which is what got the attention of the kid in the doorman's suit. Except that he wasn't a kid and it wasn't a doorman's suit, simply the friendly bank's version of a non-threatening security uniform. Gold-trimmed red seemed much cheerier than the standard authoritarian brown. Bank guard Terry McKinney didn't much care what the uniform looked like, as long as he had a job. He was lucky to have one at all—especially one where they let him carry a gun. It was a couple years now since he'd come home from Desert Storm, and the docs at the V.A. said he still wasn't right. Post-traumatic stress disorder, they said. Whatever that meant. So what if he was a little nervous? As a war veteran, he was entitled to be a little twitchy. Didn't anybody remember DeNiro in *Taxi Driver?*

Lounging outside with a cigarette, Terry heard someone bellowing like a wounded water buffalo. And reached the lobby just in time to see the bare-assed guy get beaned with the typist's dictionary.

"A sex pervert!" she shouted. "He's trying to pull out his dick!"

"A hold-up!" Tiffany corrected. "He said he's got a gun."

"What'd they say?" Clarice asked. "He needs the john?"

It was all Terry needed to hear. At last, an opportunity to show the friendly bank that Terry McKinney, war veteran, was still a man of action. He pulled out his Beretta and dropped into a combat crouch. The first seventeen rounds, fired in Alonzo's general direction, took out the overhead lights, the front windows, and a good deal of plasterboard. The would-be robber, who'd dived for the floor, was covered in plaster dust—which adhered even more now that he'd pissed himself in the face of enemy fire.

Popping in another clip, Terry let it rip. His wad-cutter ammo tore through the bank, a smoking swath of destruction. This time, the water cooler was mortally wounded, along with the fax machine and the information lady's potted ivy. By now Alonzo was crawling through the haze of exploding plaster toward the exit. Belly down to avoid the fusillade, the friendly bank's employees never noticed. The screams that echoed in the vestibule might have been their own.

Three ammo clips later, Terry was finally out of bullets. Brushing debris off his red blazer, he swaggered out to greet the cops responding to Southlawn's hold-up alarm. The one Clarice had finally remembered to activate once she'd shaken the plaster chunks out of her hair.

After taking witness statements from all the bank employees, followed by a careful examination of the crime scene, the reporting officers assessed their clues. It was easy to establish the would-be robber's identity, since Alonzo had left his wallet, his driver's license and his hundred dollars on Tiffany's desk. The cops also discovered something else that seemed in keeping with the Southlawn Bank's policy of "penalty for early withdrawal." Some important physical evidence was found in the vestibule, along with a trail of blood that continued outside to the curb, where Odell had waited in the getaway car. A single .38 caliber bullet casing was recovered in the doorway—obviously from Alonzo's revolver, which lay in the puddling blood near the other evidence:

the penis that had been shot off when his gun discharged as he crawled to safety.

Night Moves

Another Saturday night in Crime Central. That's Chicago's inner city West Side, where I work midnight shifts on "vertical patrol"—copspeak for the high-rise projects beat. Any cop will tell you this is a beat like no other. The norm here is that there is no norm—*anything* can happen and usually does. For cops and the people who live here, each night in the projects is an adventure in survival.

In Chicago, the high rise projects are located at all points on the city map. The north side is home to the infamous Cabrini Green, while the south side claims the fearsome Robert Taylor homes. Where I work, on the west side, it's Rockwell Gardens, a fanciful name for the monoliths that reach high above the inner city like grimy fingers clawing for release. Violence is the language spoken here. The clustered placement of the buildings is strategically brilliant, if you're trained in Sniping and High-Powered Weaponry. From apartments on the higher levels, a sniper can pick off a rival gang member, an innocent bystander or the windshield of a police squad without fear of detection.

In these buildings, apartments are entered from an outdoor balcony, motel-style, that spans the width of the building. A bad idea for the inner city, where too many bodies got tossed over the railings during domestic disputes, gang fights, or the boozy brawl that went too far. Which made it necessary, eventually, for the Chicago Housing Authority to add steel mesh on the balconies from ground to roof, making the buildings appear to be what their residents had felt they were all along: cages of crime and violence where staying alive is a daily struggle.

On any given night, it's the same scene. Some people loiter in front of the buildings, sharing bottles or a few joints, waiting for the random breeze to dilute the stench that's as much a part of the projects as the eroded bricks. Others lurk in the shadows, watching and waiting. These are the predators, well versed in the cardinal rule of the street: Crime, like luck, has a certain window of opportunity.

Anyone here is easy prey. Staying alive is the name of the game, one that has few rules and fewer winners. No one is exempt from the random, devastating violence, not the players or the bystanders, or even the police.

It's hard to describe what a cop feels when working a project beat. Parading whores, lizard-eyed junkies nodding over a nickel of smack, hustlers and thieves who wait in the shadows are all a part of the landscape here. Inside the buildings, it's the darkness you notice first—a perpetual gloom that comes from shot-out light fixtures, windowless halls and lobbies that look more like grim tunnels than residential buildings. Nightmare-sized vermin skitter along the walls and floors. Rank odors of human waste mix with the lingering insecticide stench, strong enough to have you choking. Coming into a building, you breathe through your mouth, creep cautiously up stairwells littered with garbage or worse. You move quickly in the dark, with only the narrow beam of your flashlight to navigate. Just answer the call, take care of business, and get out fast. This is a dangerous place for cops who come as peacemakers, but arrive as targets.

It's brutally cold tonight, with a relentless wind shrieking like an unpaid whore. The kind of weather that keeps people inside, and the streets nearly deserted. Which means an easy night for traffic cops, but a tough one for those of us who work this beat. In the projects, liquor and drugs are the common antidote for cabin fever. On nights like this, the police radio crackles all night long with an onslaught of "violence calls." Fights between neighbors, husbands vs. wives, gang against gang—all demanding police presence.

We're so busy tonight that when the call comes, there's no unit available to take it.

"Attention, all units in the Eleventh District, all units on citywide, we have a man shot at Rockwell Gardens, repeat, a man shot, Rockwell Gardens, Adams at Western Avenue. Any unit available to ride on this?"

The dispatcher's voice is pleading. He *knows* all units are busy, knows every available officer is out in the fray, hip deep in bad blood and attitude.

"Repeating that flash, we have a man shot at Adams and Western. Getting a lot of calls on this one, people. Any unit nearby that can take this call?"

When no one responds, he exercises his dispatcher's authority.

"1134, hold off on that burglar alarm job, and respond to the man shot instead. 10-4?"

We're just pulling up to a grocery store where the burglar alarm is wailing. And even though we're more than twenty blocks away from the shooting location, orders are orders.

"10-4, Squad. We're on the way." We flip on the blue lights and hit the siren, which nearly drowns out the dispatcher's last message.

"'34, use extreme caution. I have no cars to send for back-up, and callers are saying there's quite a crowd out there."

Our blue lights and siren help us traverse the district in record time, but we douse them a few blocks from our destination. No need to broadcast our arrival. There's a rhythm to working these streets—covert night moves honed from countless encounters, untold fights. No charging up like the cavalry in this parts, not if we want to stay alive. Instead, we ease into the danger zone, slip through the shadows and assess the situation before making a move.

When we pull up, there's a crowd of shouting people blocking the project's entrance. It's clearly an incendiary situation, the kind that one wrong move could escalate to full-blown riot status. Fear and hostility cut through the darkness as effectively as the howling wind. We park our squad in a copse of trees some distance from the entrance. All we know is that one man—or maybe more—has been shot, with the shooter possibly still on the scene. No telling who in this crowd might have a gun, a knife, a high-tech machine pistol loaded with Teflon ammo that can slide right through our safety vests. And there's only the two of us, two uniforms to navigate this sea of outraged faces.

This is where we "walk the walk." Game face and an authoritative stance—even when we're quaking inside—is the only thing that gets us through this crowd. We move through it quickly, carefully, reading the faces around us. We haven't drawn our guns—not yet, not with a mob like this. But ready to draw, just in case.

We find him in the darkened lobby. The people are shouting and pointing at the man who's leaning casually against the wall. Maybe too casually. Our weapons are out in an instant.

"Hands UP!" my partner screams, legs locking in a combat crouch. "Get 'em up on your head or I'll drop you right now!"

The man doesn't budge. Instead, he stares with glittering eyes while his lips move slowly, almost in slow motion pantomime.

"I'm the one been shot," he rasps, and points toward his chest with a trembling hand. There's no visible wounds, no evidence of bleeding, but his face is ashen. Those glazed eyes could mean recent drug usage or recent trauma. Cautiously, we move toward him.

He moans when we touch him, flinches as we lift his sweater. The black cable knit is damp to the touch, sodden with the blood absorbed from five spurting entry wounds that circle his heart. Five .38 caliber bullets had been pumped in—at close range, judging by the singed carbon circles on his chest. But the man is still upright, still talking. A good sign that the bullets might have missed the pericardial sac.

While my partner radios for an ambulance, the man, Andre Bridwell, tells me what happened. He'd been looking forward to this evening, he says. Saturday was payday, the only night he didn't have to work late. He'd stopped off to cash his check, and pick up some wine for later. Saturday nights meant kicking back with his woman, Chantel, the only warm spot in a cold, hard week.

When Andre got home, the candles were already lit and some smooth sexy jazz was pulsing on the radio. Chantel was waiting for him. He could hear her voice in the bedroom, that deep throaty sound that made him hunger. Slipping out of his coat and shoes, Andre grabbed the wine and headed into the bedroom.

Chantel was naked. Gilded by the candle's glow, her body was a ripe offering of gold and bronze splayed across the bed. Her lush lips were open, moist as bruised berries, and her hooded eyes glinted in the candlelight.

It was something about the candlelight, Andre recalls. The flames reflected in her eyes, just the way they glinted off the muzzle of the gun held by the man who stepped forward. The man who was Andre's brother.

Andre doesn't remember much after that. The candlelight and muzzle fire flashed together—a burst of gold light and white-hot pain as five rounds were pumped into his chest. He recalls Chantel screaming, and thudding footsteps—his own- as he stumbled out of the apartment and down to the lobby.Now Andre slumps against the wall, sweating profusely.

She must have been raped, he tells us. His brother Aaron always was a no-count jealous fool—begrudged his brother everything he had—even Chantel.

Andre reaches out a clutching hand as his eyes roll in supplication.

"You got to help her, officer. You got to take care of my woman."

But it's all we can do to take care of Andre. The wail of sirens in the distance tells us the ambulance has arrived. But in the projects, paramedics won't enter the premises unless escorted by the police. Since we're the only cops around, we'll have to walk our victim out of the building and across the 200 yards or so to the waiting ambulance rig. Which means negotiating this deadly terrain with a bleeding man while the crowds scream that it's our fault—the police who *never* show up, *never* protect the innocent people. Some people think *we* shot Andre, and their angry shouts join in the furor.

We're shoved and jostled as we push through, dragging the trembling man with us. Fear pushes up like bile in my throat, a taste as sharp as the smell of Andre's blood. Supporting his lax body, surrounded by the frenzied mobs, there's no easy way to get to our guns if someone makes a move. Nothing to do but push our way through, nothing but prayer and guts to get us out of here.

When a crying woman approaches us, we nearly push past her until Andre cries out. It's Chantel, his lover, he tells us. The woman who owns his heart. Immediately, the crowd parts to allow the sobbing woman closer.

"I thought you were dead!" she cries piteously, reaching out to Andre. Chantel hugs him tight, so close we almost don't see her plunge the knife in, pull it up in a quick, vicious thrust, finally stilling the heart that she owned.

"Motherfucker wouldn't die!" she shouts. "Shot five times and he wouldn't die."

A series of freeze-frame images followed—the gasping crowd, the repeater blast of smoke and flame as we dropped the beloved Chantel. And then the quick swivel spin—our final move in this deadly scenario—as we level 9mm bores on the advancing mob.

"First one comes closer is dead!" my partner shouts. "We'll put you down like a rabid dog! Anybody here ready to die?"

Smoke and cordite burn my eyes, sweat slicks my back. My finger strokes the trigger, and I wait for any takers.

Viewer
Discretion
Advised

Things might have been different if he hadn't interrupted her program. All week long, Darla Wick waited for Thursday night to watch "E.R." For six years she'd been a loyal fan, following the cast through their heartbreaks, romances, tragedies and triumphs. Tonight, she'd find out if Nurse Hathaway would shun Dr. Ross once and for all and finally marry that *other* guy. A man who, in her opinion, was not nearly as handsome as George Clooney, but a woman had to draw the line somewhere. What good was a handsome face if it covered a cheating heart?

On Thursday evening she was ready. Since her husband Roy was working late again, she had the house and the TV to herself. By eight o'clock, the dishes were done, the laundry folded, and Darla sat waiting in front of her forty-eight-inch screen. A single lamp illuminated the room, casting soft shadows on the velvet Elvis painting that dominated the sofa wall. Sipping diet cola, Darla fidgeted in anticipation as the show's theme music began to play.

She'd barely glimpsed the cheating Dr. Ross or any of the other characters before her front door swung open and Roy lurched into the room. Judging by the 100-proof cloud that blew in with him, it smelled like her husband was marinated in sour mash. After tripping over the ottoman, he crashed into the coffee table and sent the cola, the TV remote and a crystal bowl of chocolate candy flying, landing finally in a tangled heap on the couch.

"You clumsy jackass! Is this what you call 'working late?'" Darla hissed, scrambling to retrieve her snacks. "Getting shit-faced in some gin mill?"

"Not shit-faced," Roy belched. "We gotta talk, Darla."

"You're drunker 'n a skunk, Roy. What the hell were you up to tonight?"

"My *life,*" he said with a bleary smile. "I been getting my life together. I finally figured it out."

"In the bottom of a glass, huh? Go get in the shower- you're stinking up the furniture."

Shoving his feet off the upholstery, Darla grimaced at his reeking breath. It wasn't unusual for him to stop for a few beers sometimes, but this was a new low.

She glanced at the screen where Nurse Hathaway was discussing bridesmaids' gowns with her nurses. Damn Roy anyway! He was talking so loud he drowned out their dialog.

"Go take a shower," she repeated testily. "Don't come barreling in here all sloppy drunk and smelly and expect to get something from me." Although she couldn't remember the last time they'd had sex, it didn't bother her, particularly. The spark between them had died a long time ago. As far as she was concerned, her husband was a roommate who ate at her table and slept in her bed. The less time he spent in either place, the better.

Hiccuping again, Roy reached out a shambling hand to grip her arm.

"I'm serious, Darla. We gotta talk. I'm leaving."

"Then *go,* dammit." If he left now, she could still catch the show's remaining 45 minutes.

"I'm leaving *you,* Darla. I wanna be with somebody else."

"Uh-huh." She noticed that the red-haired female doctor had a new hairstyle, a younger, fresher look. Raking pudgy fingers through her own short hair, Darla wondered how the style would look on her.

At the commercial break, she popped another chocolate and glanced irritably at her husband. He was snoring now, deep whistling snorts that made her want to punch him. And his head was tilted back, pressing against Elvis's booted foot. There'd be hell to pay if he smeared it with any of that damn hair gel he'd been wearing lately. She nudged him, none too gently, with her fluffy slipper.

"Dammit, Ray! I told you to take your drunk ass into the shower. You're messing up Elvis!"

"Quit shovin' me, woman!" Hacking and coughing his way back to wakefulness, he glared at his wife in her orange caftan. Draped in the folds of the wild striped print, she looked like she'd been eaten by a circus tent. He couldn't remember the girl he'd married, or when she'd been replaced by this three-chinned pig. Or maybe it was just that now he had someone better to compare her to.

"Guess you didn't hear me the first time. I said I'm leavin' you, Darla."

But her eyes were glued to the screen, where Dr. Ross had finally realized that Nurse Hathaway belonged to someone else.

"Dammit, Darla!" Ray slammed his fist against the wall, a direct shot to Elvis' flowing velvet cape. "Listen to me when I talk to you. I told you I'm leaving."

"So go!" she retorted. "Leave me the hell alone so I can watch my program."

"I want a *divorce*, goddammit!"

On screen, the emergency team clustered around an injured patient, working feverishly to save him. In the reclining chair, Darla's lips were pressed in a thin tight line. Suspense over the patient's fate or reaction to Roy's latest statement? He wasn't sure. And decided, with the skewed judgement bought by too many bourbons, that it was time to 'fess up. He'd heard that confession was good for the soul. Once everything was out in the open, maybe he'd feel better.

"There's somebody else. No sense pretending this marriage is gonna work anymore, cuz we both know better." He waited, wondering why Darla didn't speak. For some reason, she seemed to be holding her breath. But at least her eyes had shifted, finally, from the screen to his face. They were thin green slits that watched him like a stalking cat.

"I didn't plan on falling in love, but some things you can't control. It just happened."

She wasn't shouting yet, which he thought was a good sign. And the tears hadn't started, so maybe she wouldn't try to lay a guilt trip. But this cold silence was the last thing he'd expected. Rubbing his chin nervously, Roy cleared his throat.

"So I figure, the best thing to do is end it now. A clean break so we can both get on with our lives, y'know?" He shrugged, sent his wife a pleading look. "I never meant to hurt you, Darla. But I think this is best for both of us."

On the screen, the bridesmaids were in the church vestibule, taking bets to see if Dr. Ross would have the nerve to show his face.

"Who is she?" The words sliced out, as sharp and deadly as a TV doctor's scalpel.

"It don't matter who it is. Just that it ain't happenin' between you and me no more." He thought he saw Darla's eyes flash fire, but he was still too tipsy to be sure.

"Who *is* she?" Tipsy or not, there was no mistaking her tone that time—hard enough to nail him to the Elvis picture. Why was it that women always had to know the details? Did it really make a difference if the outcome was the same? But after seventeen years, maybe he owed her that. Throw her a bone as he was walking out the door.

"Cassie Perkins," he admitted. And watched the green slits widen to spotlight size.

"*Cassie Perkins?* That bleached blonde bitch who cashiers at the liquor store?"

"Only on weekends. She takes classes during the week." Roy frowned, wishing he could wipe that smirk off her fat face. "She wants to be a nursing assistant."

"Perfect!" Darla snorted. "After you give me shit for seventeen years, she takes classes in cleaning it."

"Forget the remarks, okay? Can't we just be adults about this? Work it out like civilized people?" Roy watched as Darla's gaze shifted back to the TV. So far, so good, he thought. She hadn't thrown anything yet, and nobody had tossed the first punch.

On the screen, the nurse/bride waited at the church, wondering why her groom jilted her. When they cut to commercials, Darla returned her attention to Roy.

"So it's a clean break you want?" An unexpectedly calm voice.

"I think that's best." Roy tensed, waiting for the hysterics he knew would follow. But Darla surprised him again.

"I think you're right," she agreed. "For all concerned." Poking delicately through the bowl of chocolates, she selected three, wolfing them down as she heaved herself out of the chair.

He expected the delayed reaction to kick in where she'd hurl herself at him, shrieking and clawing his face. Or maybe heave a lamp in his direction—*anything* that would show her rage. In seventeen years, she'd never been a calm opponent and his body had the scars to prove it. But this time, she merely waddled off toward the bathroom.

Was it possible? Could it be that she was willing to let him go so easily? Maybe she had somebody else. No. Watching her wobble like jelly in that orange tent she wore, Roy knew that couldn't be true—not unless the guy owned stock in a chocolate factory.

He slouched back against the couch and let out a relieved sigh. Now that he'd laid his cards on the table, the rest would be easy. A few legal details, and then he and Cassie could be together. A clean break—the best way to go.

Which is exactly what Darla explained to the police who came to investigate her husband's homicide. Initially, they'd been called by a neighbor reporting the explosion that blasted out the back wall of the Wicks' mobile home. Because it was nearly ten o'clock, it was too dark for the neighbor to see what else had blown out into the yard. Specifically, the head of Roy Wick and a considerable portion of the velvet Elvis.

Officers on the scene observed the body of the late Mr. Wick, still lounging comfortably against the sofa, and the twelve-gauge shotgun propped near Mrs. Wick's recliner chair—exactly where she'd placed it while she watched the last of her program. She'd been slightly chilly by that time, due to the substantial hole in the wall, but she toughed it out anyway. It wasn't every episode that Nurse Hathaway got left at the altar and—just as Darla suspected— by the program's end the sneaky Dr. Ross was already trying to worm his way back into her heart.

As the handcuffs snapped into place, Darla told police it was too bad that television wasn't more like real life. That way, the cheating man would get exactly what he deserved. A clean break was best for everyone...especially when it made his head a lawn ornament.

The Gift

"Drop the gun."

I can barely breathe, don't dare to move a muscle. The eyes that watch me are as steady and unwavering as the gun aimed at my heart. Nothing else exists now. I can't hear the traffic outside, the muffled sounds of arguing neighbors, only the thud of my own tripping pulse.

"Put down the gun. It's not too late. We can talk about this."

Even to my own ears, my voice sounds high and shaky, strung thin in the face of this unblinking opponent. My sweaty hands clamp the waffled grips of the gun I pulled too late. Nothing to do now but pray and hope this killer grants my reprieve. I can smell the sweat of my partner behind me, feel his breath hot on my neck. There's nothing either of us can do but wait and wonder if it's death or redemption that will be handed down by the nine year old girl who points the gun.

The call came initially as "children left alone." We'd been here before, often enough to know the building and most of its inhabitants—the crack whores who lounged on the stoop outside, the junkies nodding in the dark vestibule, the old lady on the second floor who set aside her gin bottle long enough to dial 911 when she heard the kids crying.

There are five of them in this fourth-floor walk-up, all the children of Virginia Summers, part-time whore, full-time junkie, and most times abusive mom. Countless social workers have investigated the family, sometimes removing the kids to temporary shelters. But in spite of their malnutrition and obvious bruises, Virginia always manages to get them back. Children belong with their mother, she'd weep at the custody hearings. Decked out in semi-clean, respectable clothes borrowed or stolen from someone else, she'd paint such a convincing picture of maternal concern, the judges usually relented, and returned the children to Virginia's personal version of Hell.

In a household where dope is purchased in nickels and dimes, there's no such thing as grocery money, no pantry stocked with anything but the random six-pack of beer. So while Mama fixes up in the corner, sometimes nodding out with the spike still in her arm, it's up to the kids to fend for themselves. The two oldest, Mimi and Todd, are the designated family providers. Some nights, it's dumpster *du jour* that feeds the babies, tossed-out scraps that keep them quiet and fill their empty bellies. Other times, it's whatever they can steal from the local fruit stands or the neighborhood grocery. Either way, it's never enough to stop the hunger pangs, or to keep the babies from crying for long.

But Mimi tries to do her best. She knows there'll be trouble as soon as Daniel, the youngest, starts to whimper. That's all it takes for Jeffrey and Rhonda to wail along, and for Mama to start swinging—either her fists, or whatever weapon's in easy reach. She can't stand squalling brats, she tells them. And flings a pot or an empty beer bottle just to prove her point.

All five kids bear the marks of Virginia's temper. Scars and bruises cover bodies that shudder whenever Mama walks in the room. The neighbors hear it all through the paper-thin walls—the beatings, the screams, the drunken mother finally slamming down the stairs toward the next trick and the next fix. Sometimes, they look in to make sure the kids made it through the latest brawl. But most nights, they're deep in the grip of their own demons. Used syringes and broken bottles litter the building's creaky stairs, an obvious sign that the good neighbor policy can't last long.

On this warm May afternoon, it's Bernice in 2A who called the police. Sucking on toothless gums, she watches us climb the stairs, reluctantly steps out on the landing to describe what she'd heard.

"It was worse than usual this time. I heard them kids screamin', and her shoutin'. Then crashing

sounds, like she was breaking things. Poor babies."
She shakes her head sadly, enough to make her pink
sponge curlers wobble. "Women like her don't
deserve to have kids. They're gifts from God,
y'know."

"Right, Bernice. So what happened next?"

"No tellin'. I heard a real loud noise. Thought
maybe she'd slammed the door hard enough to
knock it off its hinges. Scared the bejeezus out of
me." The old lady shivers, pulling her housecoat
tighter. "I was afraid to look out. Afraid she might
come after me next."

"Did she leave then?"

"Must have. Ain't heard her screamin' no more."
This time, Bernice's quivering lip curls into a sneer.
"By now she's probably on Sheridan Road, on her
knees for a ten-dollar trick."

We continue the climb to the fourth floor. On the
landing, we can just barely hear them. The breathless
whimpers of a baby too tired or too close to death
to continue the effort. The muffled sobs of the others,
choked with fear and pain. The door of the apartment
is intact but ajar, and we sidle through cautiously.

Baby Daniel is on the floor where he was dropped
or flung with enough force to compress the side of
his skull. Little Rhonda huddles nearby, shivering in
a pool of her own urine, a two-year old's natural
response to terror. Seven year old Todd shrinks back

against the wall, shielding Jeffrey, aged three. Both boys's faces are pulped with bruises that swell their eyes nearly closed. At the sight of us, Jeffrey starts to wail anew.

"Shhhhh, it's okay now. We're gonna help you. Don't worry, baby." Every instinct has me reaching out to comfort him, draw them all in a circle of protection too late. But his arm is hanging at an odd angle, another gift from his loving Mom, and I don't dare touch him before the paramedics arrive.

"Jesus Christ!" my partner mutters behind me. "I hope the heartless bitch fries in hell."

Vermin scurry over the filthy floor, scattering only when our footsteps approach. The room is strewn with garbage, broken bottles, soiled clothes heaped in piles. The stench today is worse than usual, layered with a sickly-sweet odor of something else.

Four of the Summers' kids are here with us, which leaves only Mimi unaccounted for.

Mimi, the nine year old and surrogate mom. Mimi who levels the gun when we step into the kitchen.

Contrary to the neighbor Bernice's report, Virginia Summers didn't slam out the door.

And she can't possibly be on her knees on Sheridan Road, not when she's slumped against the kitchen wall with a seeping entry wound at center mass. The green blouse she wears is soaked with red, enough to leak in thickening rivulets across the linoleum floor.

Although Mimi's lip is cracked and bleeding, she holds it firm, daring us to make a move. I can see us reflected in her frightened eyes, two cops frozen in this grisly tableau. It's heart that has her holding the gun, heartbreak what makes her shoulders tremble.

"Put the gun down, honey," I whisper. "It's okay. Nobody's going to hurt you anymore. I promise." The little girl's eyes are swimming now, a prelude to the sobs that follow. When the gun clatters to the floor, she allows me to gather her in my arms.

Rocking her, I hold her until there are no more tears, until she can finally recount the day's events. How she and Todd earned money by running errands—eight whole dollars. Today was a special day, she explains, and they'd wanted to surprise Mama. A surprise that consisted of the ingredients for a family dinner—chicken, a box of rice, and enough milk for all the babies.

She thought Mama would be happy. Instead, she went crazy. Accused the kids of stealing her drug money as she flung the groceries against the wall. Daniel was next, slammed so hard he couldn't even scream.

Mimi recalls how the cries of her brothers and sister were echoing in her head. Daniel wasn't moving and Mama wouldn't stop, striking out like a madwoman. She doesn't remember when she got the gun—only the way Mama's eyes widened just after she pulled the trigger. Then, nothing but wispy smoke and trickling blood.

We take the children away long before the body is removed. Transport them via ambulance to the hospital, where they'll get treatment and food and much-needed baths.

And notice, as we shuttle through the waiting room, a newspaper left by some other visitor.

There's a half-page ad in bold type, trumpeting the occasion of this special day: "May 14th is Mother's Day. Do something nice for the mother you love."

Clothes Make
the Man

It's three a.m. when the call is broadcast: a burglary that just occurred at the clothing store. According to the citizen who called it in, four young males were seen fleeing on foot from Chauncey's Lords of Style. We're just a few blocks from the place—a pricey boutique frequented by high-rolling dope dealers, pimps and anyone else who dresses for success in orange silk suits and sequined bikini underwear. By the time we roll up to the store, a marked squad is on the scene and two uniformed guys are beginning their preliminary investigation. Since we're an unmarked unit, we'll cruise around, checking out the surrounding area.

This particular part of Uptown is a long seedy stretch of pawn shops, liquor stores, and country bars. It's also a stroll for the whores and dealers until the bars close at two, by which time most of the street people have gotten high, drunk or hustled, and gone to wherever they call home for the night. Other than the winos slumped in the doorways, there are few people out at this time of morning. Which makes the slim young man standing near the mailbox all the more conspicuous. He's not more than twenty, and judging by the waist level view we have of him, a slender build, maybe a hundred and thirty-five pounds stretched out on a six-foot frame. Even in the dim street light, we can see how his white T-shirt is plastered to his ribcage, and his face is bathed in sweat. He's leaning against that mailbox, working on calm, but his chest is heaving.

"Step away from the mailbox and get on the wall." In perfect sync, my partner and I are out of the car with weapons drawn. The kid gapes at us but doesn't move.

"I didn't do nothin'."

"Then you won't care if we search you. Get on the wall."

Staring at the twin bores of our 9 millimeters can be a strong persuader. His eyes widen, lips move in a last snarling attempt at bravado as he starts to comply.

"Why you hasslin' me? I just come out here to mail a damn letter!"

"And decided to hug the mail box for awhile? Making a special delivery?"

When he steps to the wall we get our first full length view of him. For a skinny guy, his ass is the size of the Titanic's anchor. At least four axe-handles across, by conservative estimate, there's so much of it he can barely move. Like a rodeo rider after a bad day at the bull pen, he walks stiff-legged without bending his knees. Even with the current street fashion trend of oversized baggy jeans, this is clearly overkill.

"What's your name?"

"Cornelius Jones."

"What's up with the pants, Cornelius?"

"Nuthin'."

"Looks a little bottom-heavy to me."

Cornelius is starting to tremble, but he stills tries to run his game.

"Big asses run in my family. On my mother's side."

My partner steps back while I do the search. Patting the back pockets, I feel nothing.

No concealed weapons, no contraband...and no body. There's no tactile indication of a person underneath—only more jeans. When I pull back the waistband, I see them—more waistbands of more jeans—so many they circle his waist like a denim inner tube. The smell of sweat and wet fabric sizing rises up around us.

"How come you got so many pairs of jeans on, man?"

"Uh, er, uh... My girlfriend like a big booty. If I don't wear my drawers like this, she think I'm too skinny."

"She like you to wear the price tags too?" The tags from Chauncey's Lords of Style that Cornelius forgot to remove, and that are now his ticket to jail.

At the station, Cornelius peels off his stolen jeans—twenty pairs in all. When the last pair comes off, he looks like a just-plucked chicken. Quaking in billowing boxer shorts, he's ready to talk. And like many first-time arrestees, once he starts talking, he spills his guts.

It seemed like a great idea, he tells us. Chauncey's sells high-end designer jeans with hundred-dollar price tags. Why not boost a stack of them to fence on the street? He could make a bundle. While his partners aimed for the store safe and cash register, Cornelius had other plans—just a quick in-and-out for the clothes. But once inside the store though, he realized he hadn't brought anything to carry the proceeds. The bags used for store customers were too small and flimsy—not practical for hauling stacks of heavy jeans. So he came up with what seemed a practical solution. He'd *wear* them out, a better idea since it wouldn't arouse suspicion if he was seen on the street.

Starting with his normal size—a 28-inch waist—Cornelius slipped into the first pair. After a couple pairs, he'd switch to the next size, ending finally with a size 40. All of them were designer labels, all made of heavyweight denim with multiple cargo pockets.

Stylish when wearing a single pair, crippling when there's twenty. He could barely move. His knees wouldn't bend, and each step felt like he was dragging lead weights. And when he tried to run, he thought he'd have a heart attack. Hoofing it down Broadway, he figured he sweat out at least ten pounds of water weight.

Because the proceeds of the crime total two thousand dollars, Cornelius is booked on felony charges. And since he's waived the right to an attorney, he agrees to sign his confession, reading over his typed statement only long enough to tell us there's an error.

"You forgot the drawers," he says.

"Twenty pairs of jeans, Cornelius. It's all there."

"No, man. I mean the *drawers*. The underwear!"

Underwear?

It seems that Cornelius was not without a certain fashion aesthetic. While ripping off the jeans, he'd decided that style was important, inside and out. And helped himself to a display of designer undies— bikinis, thongs and male g-strings—in a dazzling array of silk and sequins.

So many fabrics and colors he couldn't decide, so he took them all. Tossed them into a plastic garment bag and hit the street.

"So what'd you do with them, Cornelius? Stash 'em somewhere?"

Frowning, his eyes move to the wall clock.

"Don't matter," he says sheepishly. "It's too late."

"What's too late?"

"It's five o'clock, man. That mail box on Broadway gets emptied at four."

Bird of Prey

I smell him before I see him. An odor best described as "dumpster funk"—cheap booze, reeking body and fetid breath- steeped together in one killer stench that precedes the shambling steps behind me. His white cane taps out a blind man's awkward cadence on the sidewalk, followed by the shuffle-drag of crippled feet. But this is no sightless senior citizen hobbling through the last miles of his life. This is a vicious rapist, and I'm his next victim.

Dubbed "the blind man rapist" by our tactical team, his M.O. is simple. He strikes in the twilight hours, after the rush hour crowd has dwindled. Once darkness descends, but before an hour that would arouse suspicion of a handicapped old man who lingers on the streets, he taps along near bus stops and street corners that are conveniently close to darkened areas. Playlots with dense groupings of bushes and trees, dimly lit alleys and park property have all been crime scenes for his previous victims— seven so far. Only five survived his brutal attacks.

According to past victims, he's consistent in his approach. Playing on their sympathy, he wobbles along, pausing uncertainly at a traffic signal or bus stop. A convincing performance, they said, since every step looked to be his last. And when they offered assistance to someone who they assumed was a pathetic old man, he accepted gratefully, adding that he'd somehow gotten lost. And then requested "just a little help" in crossing the street, or negotiating a corner. They even took his arm, they said, guiding him along until he was sure no one was nearby and his cover was secure.

Most victims were bound with rope that left deep, raw ligature marks at throat and wrists. Underwear was sliced off and taken as "trophies" by the same knife he used to penetrate them, an act of savagery that was the prelude to the cane and finally, his own thrusting release. Afterward, some of the victims were stabbed, almost as an afterthought. Those who survived recounted how he'd stood there above them, eyes glazed and oddly expressionless, fondling the blade of his knife.

Now he trails me down this dim street, anticipating how he'll carve me like a helpless bird. Tonight, I'm the predator disguised as prey. A tough transition for a street cop with years of experience in "walking the walk." My instincts dictate I rip his throat out. Instead, I play the helpless female—an anonymous Jane Doe in sensible pumps and conservative clothes. The defenseless working girl as Victim #8.

I lead him past a neon-washed strip—drug store, currency exchange, barber shop—all closed at this hour but still flickering light on the deserted street. Not enough to spook him—just to provide a clear visual for my backup posted down the block.

I pause, considering the steps that lead up to the El platform. By all appearances, I could be heading up to catch my train, a convincing part of my working girl act. I'd love to lure him to the platform, make him do his crippled routine up thirty five steep steps. And finally, when he makes his move, I'd watch the bastard fry when my back-up tosses him on the third rail. A perverse impulse and an unprofessional one. As a cop, it's my duty to deliver him to the legal forms of justice. As a woman, I can't help but think of other options.

We stop at the corner. There's an alley beyond it, and dense six-foot hedges that circle a deserted playground. Near the playground entry is a standard Park District restroom—a small brick building with a doorless shadowed tunnel that separates the two facilities—the perfect cover for a violent crime. The blind rapist steps closer.

He's next to me now, clutching feebly at the cane he taps in small circles. The smell of him gags me, the proximity of this beast is enough to knot my roiling stomach, but I turn to him with a questioning smile. My reflections dance in the thick lenses of his dark-tinted glasses, and I know he's gauging me, waiting to reel me in. Anticipating the hand I hold out, my polite offer to help. I want to drop him like a rabid dog. Instead, I allow him to place my hand under his arm.

In every cop's experience, there are moments when we shudder and cringe, when our hearts and brains and souls scream out that *nothing* is worth some things we have to do, no amount of money could ever compensate for certain deeds. Usually those are moments involving hurt kids, or crime scenes so horrendous they'd have to be modified to qualify for mere nightmare status.

Tonight, touching this animal is one of those moments.I hold his arm—the one that gutted his victims?—and wonder which pocket holds the rope. Watch his steps become more agile as we approach the hedges and imagine—hope- that he pulls his weapon first. Will my backup have a clear shot?

My heart is tripping double-time, the adrenaline rush before show time. The arm I hold tightens against his ribcage to lock my hand in place as his cane clatters to the pavement. When his hand delves into his jacket I'm ready. Ready to pull him into a throw while sweeping his legs before he ever gets the rope out, or the knife. *Not* ready for the compact taser he slams against my arm, zapping me with enough voltage to knock me off my feet.

I don't remember anything else. Not the arrival of my backup or the Mass Transit K-9 unit that spots us from the El platform above. I don't get to witness the pleasure of the snarling Rottweiler who corners the "blind man," or the way he begs for mercy when my partners slap on the cuffs. Later they'll show me the other weapons, his knife and rope and the straight-razor found in his shoe.

The "blind old man" is just 37 years old, recently divorced, and, according to his claims, a born-again Christian. After his interrogation, the detectives tell me what we already know, that his attorneys will try for an insanity plea. Since he's positively ID'd by four of the victims, we've got a good case. At least the rapist is off the street, they tell me, and facing some serious jail time. Somehow, it's not enough.

The Price

GINA GALLO

"....soon as I pinned that badge on, I thought I had it made. The power, the respect, excitement, and a non-stop parade of women - I wanted it all. Been through two wives, a family, and a drinking problem. The bottle's the only thing that hasn't left me. And just like before, I want something I don't have. Only this time, it's peace. From this end, the view's a lot different. I didn't believe that when I signed up. None of us did. You never think it'll happen to you."

A retired Chicago police officer, reflecting on his 30 year career-
January 14, 1991

Gunfight at
K.O. Corral

It was puckered asshole time again. Barely a few hours since his last fix and already the cramps were starting, which meant that scumbag Cisco had ripped him off again. Damn dope-dealers were all alike— jive-talking, slick-walking, lowlife slime balls who knocked down a heroin mix so much it was probably mostly milk sugar pumping through his veins tonight. Things were so bad, you couldn't even buy a decent dime bag anymore. No wonder he was already starting to jones.

Shivering, Jimmy Ray looked in the mirror. With a few upgrades, he might pass for dead. His skin was gray and clammy, a prelude to the sweats. He didn't want to think about what came after that. He couldn't. But since he'd spent his last dime on that bogus hit, there was nothing to prevent it unless...

He dug around under the soiled mattress until he found the gun, a starter pistol used in his last hold-up. It'd been dark then and the old lady hadn't known the difference. She'd given up her purse, her jewelry—

and probably would've thrown in her kidneys if he'd asked for them. People got downright cooperative when they were on the wrong end of a gun muzzle. Only problem was, the proceeds hadn't been much. Besides the rosary, peppermint lozenges, and plastic rain bonnet, the lady's purse had contained only six dollars and a senior citizen bus pass. Since the ride Jimmy Ray needed cost considerably more, he'd try something different this time, where the proceeds would be worth his trouble. A convenience store or—better yet—a neighborhood tavern. Someplace dark and smoky, with half-bagged customers drunk enough so their reflexes and coordination were shot to hell. He knew just the place. It was a little joint just a few blocks over, so small there wasn't even a sign outside. But he'd noticed that plenty of guys went in there, lumbering oafs with beer guts and bleary eyes. Just what he was looking for. But he had to hurry. The cramps were getting worse.

"Don't tell me that's silicone!" Cragin scoffed, squinting at the flickering screen. "Those are real tits if I ever saw 'em."

"That's the problem. You never seen 'em!" Feeney reached for the peanuts, which tonight were only semi-stale. "Wouldn't know a real tit if it smacked you in the face."

"I think that happened one time," Hicks chortled.

"But then your poor mother died of fright."

"Fuck you," Cragin said absently. How was he supposed to pass the titty test with some morons busting his balls? There were six of them on the barstools—tac cops who'd just finished their tour of duty and were now hunkered down at the Corral. It was their favorite cop hang-out in Area 5, equipped with the only amenities police required—a widescreen TV, a satellite dish and plenty of ashtrays. After a rough night, it was their sanctuary, a private place to unwind without interruption from the outside world. Since Gus the owner/bartender was an ex-cop himself, he understood what they needed. In the Corral, he'd created a yuppie-free zone with no fancy decor, no outside signs, nothing that looked remotely citizen-friendly. Only oldies played on the jukebox, and there wasn't a single bottle of designer water or micro-brew in sight. It was strictly a shot-and-beer joint, as rough and as solid as the cops of Area 5.

Tonight it was filled with the regulars who were watching the Finnish women's wrestling championship. Thanks to Gus' satellite dish, the broadcast came direct from Helsinki. Nobody cared that they couldn't understand a word of what the animated Finnish sportscaster was babbling. They came to the Corral for R & R, and—on good nights—a little T & A. Dialog was optional.

Down the bar, Tenorio tossed back another shot of Stoli and pointed at the screen.

"See that one in the red? Now her tits are real. Look how they jiggle every time she gets slammed. That's what I call nice."

Hicks pushed back his empty glass and signaled Gus for another.

"Hell, with a mug like that, she better have *something* nice. Her face could scare the stink off shit."

"That ain't the one we're talkin' about anyway," Cragin said. "It's this one here in the half-nelson. Wearin' the purple."

All eyes focused on the skimpy spandex outfit.

"Looks real to me." Sucking foam off his glass, Stoller nodded judiciously. "But then, she could have those saline pillow things they use now instead of silicone. S'posed to look and feel so real, you can't tell the difference. I seen a show about it on cable."

Feeney's nuts paused midway to his mouth.

"Saline? You mean saltwater? Like a fish tank?"

"You're thinkin' about the *other* end," Pankus snickered.

"I *heard* that!" From a table near the jukebox, Sergeant Natalie Oakes flipped him the bird. She considered lobbing some popcorn at him for good measure, but decided against it. It tasted pretty good tonight. For once Gus hadn't burned it.

"Hey, Pankus," she called. "Know why your dick

has a hole on the end? So you can keep an open mind!" While the rest of the females in the bar hooted, he raised his glass in salute.

"You know what the blind man said when he passed the fishmarket? 'Hello, girls!'"

"You're nothing but class and style, Pankus."

"That's why you love me, Nats."

Shaking her head, the red-haired sergeant wandered over to the jukebox.

Back at the bar, Cragin and Stoller had moved on to nipples.

"...and after they heal, if the implant went in crooked, the nipples are off-center. I seen strippers like that once at a joint on Rush Street." Stoller nodded with the authority of a lifelong mammophile. "I gotta tell ya, it was the weirdest thing I ever saw. Tits like rocks, and the nipples over on the sides, like they'd slid down or something."

"Sounds like my wife," put in Gus, setting down another round. "Only on her, *everything* slid down, especially her ass."

The men barely heard him. The Finnish wrestler in red had just executed a racy wide-angle leg lock, a move that demanded their undivided attention. At the jukebox, Natalie was punching buttons, and the Village People boomed out "Macho Man."

It was the usual nightly din, which may be why nobody noticed him at first. Sidling through the door, Jimmy Ray stood against the wall, reading the crowd. There were almost thirty of them, he figured, and from the looks of things, they'd been drinking for a while. Exactly what he wanted. This would be an easy heist. Just pull the gun, grab the money, and a half hour from now, he'd be fixing up with some primo dope. His shaking hand slipped into his jacket.

From his corner stool, Tenorio scoped the jittery kid. He was tall and skinny, early 20's, with a look the cop had seen enough times to know exactly what it meant. The edgy eyes and quivering lips were a dead-giveaway, even if he'd hidden the tracked arms. The kid was a junkie—another member of the I.V. League. Judging by the way he scanned the crowd, he hadn't come in to ask for directions.

"Mope at seven o'clock," Tenorio muttered to Hicks on his left. The other cop barely nodded. The signal passed quietly down the bar, a move as subtle as those they practiced on the street.

Cragin's eyes never left the TV screen.

"Damn shame when we can't even have a beer in peace," he observed to Gus.

"Like working overtime, only we don't get paid," Stoller agreed. His thumb flipped open the holster snap near his waistband. "Check out the muscles on the blonde in the green. Don't tell me she's not taking steroids."

"Maybe she's a switch-hitter." Beneath his jacket, Feeney already gripped his 9 mm. "They're real big on those sex-change operations over there."

"That's the *Swedish,* you mutt." Pankus wondered if there was time to finish his beer before he'd have to shoot somebody.

"Swedish, Finnish, what's the difference? They all feel the same in the dark." Gus smiled blandly. Behind the bar, his 44 Magnum was ready to go.

At the jukebox, the Village People segued into the Stones. While Mick Jagger whined about getting no satisfaction, Jimmy Ray decided to make his move. Yanking out his starter pistol, he locked his arms in an awkward TV version of a bad-ass firing stance— Barney Fife as the Evil Menace.

"This is a hold-up!" he yelled. But above Jagger's nasal moan, he could barely hear himself. Clearing his throat, he tried again. He'd moved to the center of the room, circled on three sides by cops. By now, they'd turned their attention—reluctantly—away from the wrestling Finns and toward his quivering gun. Slick with sweat, his hands could barely hold the grip.

"I mean it!" Jimmy Ray shouted. "I'll kill the first person who tries anything. Get your hands up and your wallets out."

Leaning against the jukebox, Natalie nearly smiled. The dumb kid had no idea how much shit he'd just stepped into.

"Maybe you'd like to re-think this," she told the twitching Jimmy Ray. "Believe me when I tell you this is not a real smart move."

His eyes—and pistol—shifted to the smirking redhead.

In spite of his pistol, she didn't look particularly scared. Instead, she simply arched one eyebrow and took another swallow of her beer. In fact, none of them seemed overly concerned. Exactly how drunk were these people? Gnawing his lip, he tried not to grimace. The cramps were getting worse.

"Shut up, bitch, or you'll get it first," he told her.

"I don't think so, pal." The crooning male voice was just behind his ear, a prelude to the gun pressed into his back.

"Now turn around, asshole, and see what kinda party this is." With one hand gripping a skinny shoulder, Tenorio turned Jimmy Ray to face the bar.

Gun bores, at least twenty of them, were aimed at his shaking body. From his perspective they looked like cannons. The voice in his ear was now a taunting growl.

"Ever been in a cop bar before?"

"C-c-c-cops? Oh, *shit!*"

"*No* shit!" Hicks corrected, holstering his weapon.. He picked up his beer and toasted Jimmy Ray. "Welcome to the Corral, genius."

From the jukebox, the Beatles agreed that happiness was a warm gun. Somehow, the music and the smoke twined together, choking Jimmy Ray. The cramps were like a vise now. And when the room began to spin, he was certain he'd bought the farm. His knees were already starting to buckle.

"Hey, wait a minute. This is a friggin' starter pistol." Pankus jerked it away and displayed it to the crowd. "The stupid mope didn't even bring a real gun!"

"Figures. He looks like the cap-gun type." Bored now, Feeney reached for the nuts.

"Maybe I should show him what a *real* gun can do." The 9mm ground deeper against the boy's spine. It was all Jimmy Ray needed. Like a pinball machine on tilt, his eyes rolled back just before he slumped to the floor.

At the bar, the cops resumed their scrutiny of the Finnish lady wrestlers. By squinting just a little, Cragin swore he could see an off-center nipple.

Chair Jockeys

On the street, they're called "chair jockeys." Formerly gangbangers who ran with the pack, they received a sentence no governor can commute. Some were stabbed, others beaten, many the target of an enemy bullet. Now their crippled legs are useless, arms that once cradled guns are withered and bent. The rest of their lives will be spent in wheelchairs— a bleak future served up by a violent past.

For some, it's a tough transition. They'd vowed gang allegiance until death, but nobody anticipated this other death—a living death where nothing remains but nightmares and pain. Now there's no gang brotherhood, no companionship, and no respect. Better to go out in a rage of blood and glory than the endless defeat that a wheelchair brings.

There are chair jockeys all along the North side streets of Humboldt Park. For the gangs who run these streets, they're sometimes used for storage and hiding. What better place to stash some drugs, or the smoking gun from a recent shooting than beneath the blanket of a pathetic cripple? Most cops in pursuit of the bad guys won't stop to search a wheelchair.

Other chair jockeys serve as look-outs for the drug dealers. Positioned at strategic corners, they'll watch the streets during drug sales, sounding the call when police are near.

"Five-O," they'll chant, a sound that ripples down the street from chair to chair, alerting the dealers and buyers alike. Compared to past glory days of running with a gang, the look-out gig is a lowly one. For some chair jockeys, it's a way to feel useful. For others, it's a bitter reminder of their current condition.

The man known as "J-dog" is one of the latter. Now twenty-four, he looks forty and feels even older, with lifeless legs concealed by a blanket. He'd been a gangbanger back in the day, before a stray bullet bought him life in a chair. Since then, his gang allegiance is replaced by rage, his macho pride by bitterness. These days, he prefers to live in the shadows. Darkness is the only place to hide what he's become.

We pull up to the curb, two undercover cops on a mission, and wait in the dark sanctuary provided by some ancient elms. A low whistle, barely perceptible over the rustling leaves, precedes the narrow shadow that moves from the mouth of the alley. It's J-dog who approaches us. J-dog, former gangster, current police snitch.

We lower the car window and listen. In the dark, we can barely see him but it doesn't matter. The important thing is the stream of information that begins in a low murmur of accented English. J-dog is one of our most reliable snitches.

Tonight, he talks about a recent drive-by. His voice is low but urgent, reciting a litany of names and places. Important that we catch these animals, he tells us. This time, it wasn't 'bangers who were gunned down. Of the three victims, two small children were cut down in the spray of random fire, one who was held in her mother's arms.

We record the information carefully—street intelligence to be used by the Gang Crimes Unit to find and arrest the shooters.

What J-dog doesn't tell us is that he's developed a strategy of his own. Or that the mother and baby who were gunned down were his wife and daughter, and he intends to exact his own revenge. This time, he's not concerned about consequences. As long as he sends those demons to hell, he doesn't care what happens to him. It's one of the few principles he still embraces from his gang days: pain for pain, blood for blood, life for life. For J-dog, life in a wheelchair is no life at all. But without his family, it's hell on earth.

Three weeks later, J-dog is ready. His years on the street have taught him the cardinal rule of payback: revenge is a dish best eaten cold. Tonight he'll exact his.

At seven o'clock, he wheels his chair down Division street, bound for Quinones' Memorial Chapel—a funeral parlor that caters to the gang crowd. In their business, death is big money, and the brief life span of gang members keeps the cash rolling in. On this night, the chapel is draped in swaths of gold and black—colors of the Death's Disciples gang. One of their foot soldiers is waked here, a fifteen year old boy marked by gunfire and gang tattoos. The narrow casket is draped in Disciple colors, the deceased dressed in full gang attire, with his hand curled around a handgun to protect him in the next life.

The small chapel is crowded. Enforcers are posted throughout the premises, heavily armed to discourage enemy invasion. Lines of mourners surge through the lobby and onto the street, where the gang's youngest members stand sentry, watching for rival gangs. When J-dog approaches, the crowd parts to let him pass. He's a chair jockey, a former member of their own set come to pay his respects. The proper thing to do, even for a crippled player.

In spite of the chapel's subdued lighting, the garish gang colors assault the eyes. Flowers, ribbons, lengths of fabric in relentless black and bold yellow adorn the walls, the doors, even the poster-sized pictures of the dead boy stationed around the room. In each photo he's smiling, flipping gang signs, holding a gun. Larger-than-life images that celebrate his wasted life, glorify his early death. Only the face in the casket is subdued.

The Disciples' three leaders lounge near the casket. In gang terms, they are the Chief Emon, the Kaaba, and the Emir—the three highest offices of the Disciples' hierarchy. Adorned with the ornate jewelry that comes with their positions, they pose and posture for the crowds as though the mourners have gathered in their honor.

J-dog rolls slowly toward them. The blood of his family is on their hands. These are the men who order the Disciples' actions. Because of their whims his daughter will remain a baby forever. Tonight they'll pay the price.

Placing his hand on the gleaming coffin, J-dog considers the victim within. Hardly more than a kid, just like most of those who are gunned down. In gang life, it's the foot soldiers who are expendable. They do the dirty work, pay the price as he'd done, as they all did eventually, in wars without victors fought on street corner battlefields.

It's the Chief Emon who notices J-dog first. He can barely hide his smirk. Funerals seemed to bring them out, these chair jockeys. Useless crips returning to the gang fold, if only for a night. Here was another poor bastard who wanted to feel like he still belonged. Too bad he was out of the set, but it couldn't be helped. It's part of the life, part of the code. With all the youngbloods coming up, no use shedding tears for the old and weak.

When J-dog rolls closer, the Chief Emon looks away. He can't be bothered speaking to a cripple. As the leader, the symbol of strength, he has an image to maintain. Sympathy is a sign of weakness, one he can't afford to display. What would his assembled soldiers think?

Later, the mourners who fill the chapel will recall the smell, a confusing blend of hot smoke and sweet flowers. And the way flames spat from J-dog's gun, made all three leaders leap and twitch in a macabre death dance. Others, shocked that a crippled man could operate such a powerful weapon, will simply stare at the carnage—another gruesome color added to the gang palette.

For the enforcers alerted by the sound of gunfire, their protection is too little, too late. Beside their leaders' shredded bodies sits the chair jockey, who looks oddly serene with the gun on his lap and the needle in his arm. The one that pumped in enough heroin to bring escape, redemption and freedom in one convenient hit.

After The
Smoke Clears

Most cops in Chicago's Police Department know very little about our Gang Crimes Unit. And, if asked to describe our job function, they'd probably mutter something about chasing gangbangers, or staking out low-riders to catch a glimpse of the current gang king pins, or doing damage control. We should be so lucky.

The Gangs Crimes Unit is comprised of roughly three hundred and fifty officers, hand-picked by our unit commander. We work in uniform and "soft clothes," in a tactical capacity and on covert assignment. Whenever trouble breaks out anywhere in Chicago and a strong police presence is required, they send us. We're the unit that mops up the garbage, and gets sent to trouble spots citywide to pick up the slack when the patrol units aren't enough.

We're used for street enforcement, conducting searches, raids, serving warrants, assisting the Feds, like the FBI and the DEA and anywhere else angels fear to tread. Riot control, narcotics stings, even bodyguard details for visiting dignitaries—we've done it all. Every night is something different.

The results of what we do is sent as intelligence to the Detective Division. Out on the street, undercover, we're doing the street stops, finding the guns and the dope, looking for the shooters and the killers.

And, just so nobody's confused, we *also* work with gangs. In a city that has over 300 gangs (numbers that grow each day), that means gathering intelligence, keeping up with the new crews coming in, and infiltrating, when we can, to bust up their primary source of revenue, which is narcotics.

It's a job that Hollywood always glamorizes when they crank out yet another cop action flick. On the big screen, it's portrayed by lots of fast cars, preferably expensive imported sports models, and faster women (more imported models). Heavy on the luxurious penthouses and glittery jewelry. And in the end, the good guys always win. But in a gang cop's experience, real life does *not* always imitate art. The bad guys win, or escape, and sometimes the good guys don't get a chance to ride off into the sunset. There are plenty of times when fear and doubt are the emotions *du jour*—feelings that have to be stifled because the bad guys can smell it on you. And you're shaking inside, praying that if you make it out alive, just this once, you'll never get in this situation again. But of course you do, the next day, and the day after that, because you're a cop. And that's what gang cops do.

I experienced all of those feelings during one particular incident that *Miami Vice* might have used for an episode. After six months of hard work, surveillance and intelligence gathering, my partner Phil had established a fragile relationship with the Insane Gangster Demons, a particularly vicious North Side gang. Posing as an eccentric Puerto Rican pimp and gangster, Phil was able to arrange a meeting with the middle men of a notorious Jamaican gun dealer. Affecting the accent he'd spent weeks perfecting, he told them he was in the market for sub-machine guns, preferably a compact design that featured sound suppressors and laser sights. He wanted one hundred of them, he said, as well as a couple crates of LAW rockets (anti-tank weapons) if the price was right. The mediators were impressed.

After a few more meetings and much negotiation, a bargain was struck. For the agreed price, Phil would have his weapons. But he wanted more. A transaction of this magnitude, he told them, meant that he should be treated with respect. And respect meant he would be allowed to deal with the *main man* instead of the flunkies. More meetings and negotiations, and finally, an agreement. Phil could meet the main man, *if* he brought him his best whore as a business perk, an act of good faith. Sometimes it paid to mix business with pleasure.

Phil was quick to agree. His bitches were the best, he assured them, personally trained by him to please a man in every way. He'd be happy to bring one. (He was also bringing six other people, in the form of Gangs Unit back-up teams, but he figured he'd save that surprise until later.) It was a risky set-up, but if it worked, we'd bring down one of the biggest gun suppliers in the country. If it didn't...we chose not to think about that possibility.

On the night of the big meet, Phil was decked out in a pastel linen pimp's suit and an elaborate Panama hat. He'd purposely cultivated a pencil thin mustache to complement the look, and with his natural olive skin, courtesy of his Mexican heritage, he definitely could pull it off.

As his selected "whore" and primary back-up, I had other problems. As a fair-skinned redhead, I'd never pass for a Hispanic tart. A black wig would work, but how could I conceal a Beretta 9 mm in a dress that was nothing more than an ambitious belt? Concealing a weapon is always hard when you're undercover, but the only place I had to hide a gun with this particular outfit would have required surgery to remove it. I decided, finally, to go for the Gothic Punk look, heavy on the leather and studded dog-collar. Which meant that high leather boots would complete the look and conceal my weapon.

I barely recognized myself. Black rimmed eyes, wild black wig that curled down my back like a punk Medusa. Torn fishnet stockings, a scrap of a red leather dress and a stick-on Scorpion tattoo. In this outfit, no one would make me for a cop.

We drove to the agreed meeting place on Warren Boulevard. The starless sky provided cover for the night creatures who hovered in the shadows. Pushers, whores and hustlers were out in numbers, doing a brisk business. The boulevard had been classy in its day, with grand Victorian houses and flawless gardens. But urban blight had claimed it, and the former residents were chased away by the vultures who followed, bringing crime, drugs and death.

When our car stopped at the designated address, the street people melted back into the darkness, but only until they saw the strutting pimp and his wild-haired whore step onto the sidewalk. It was just two more like them, nothing to worry about.

Entering the building's filthy vestibule, we gagged. The stench of filth, urine and steeping garbage was overwhelming. Before pressing the second floor apartment's cracked buzzer, Phil slid his Browning automatic to the back of his waistband.

"We're up there fifteen minutes," he whispered. "Then our second team comes up. The third and fourth teams will cover the outside."

I glanced up toward the dim stairwell.

"How many up there?"

"Four. The big guy and his three goons. He travels light."

"You hope." Already my knees were starting to shake.

"I *know*. He just wants to collect his money and get some ass." He glanced pointedly at my shrink-wrapped outfit as he pressed the buzzer. "Just strut around for him, let him think he's gonna get lucky. There should be no reason to go for your gun. Let them believe we're here to party. Fifteen minutes later, we'll have 'em all in handcuffs."

Heavy footsteps from somewhere above us began their descent. When I saw the body attached to those feet, I began to pray for a miracle. We'd need one if we were going to make it out of this alive.

The man who greeted us was dressed in black—voluminous, flowing fabric large enough to be an airplane tarp. His close-set eyes were glazed, indicating a recent close encounter of the narcotic kind. And they moved over me, from lips to breast and lower, like greedy sucking leeches. His evil grin featured two gold teeth that glowed like high-beams, showing little mirth and even less welcome.

"Dis da bitch?" he asked Phil in a singsong Jamaican accent. His tongue slid like a fat slug over thick dried lips.

Phil's voice slipped effortlessly into an island accent worthy of San Juan. "This girl, Melvin, she gonna blow your mind! She know how to do you right. This one could jump-start a dead man!" Joining in the man's lewd laughter, Phil winked and nudged him companionably. A seemingly casual move that told him Melvin wore no sidearms.

With sweat dripping down his face, Melvin nodded. His eyes never left my breasts. Nodding to the stairs, he motioned us forward. As I slipped past him, he leaned over, sniffing like a dog. "Save some of that for me," he growled, splashing sweat on my bare shoulder. The man was huge—big enough to freelance as a large appliance. I shuddered. It was going to be a very long fifteen minutes.

Upstairs, we discovered there were three of them, three large men with the dull-eyed expressions of the simple-minded or the very stoned. These were the mediators, the same men Phil had met with over the past months. Their clothes were wrinkled and filthy, reeking of body odor that was nearly over-powered by the stench of the garbage heaped around the room. A single lamp lit the room, barely, casting murky shadows where roaches skittered and feasted on the food remnants that littered the floor. The bathroom, with it's soiled floor, indicated that the plumbing was not in working order, and the men had obviously found a way to make do with a substitute "facility"—in this case, a stained and sodden bare mattress slung into a corner.

In the center of the room, a small folding table held the "party refreshments": a mound of cocaine on a dusty mirror, a glass-tubed pipe, a fat plastic bag of marijuana, and enough cheap wine for a good head start on cirrhosis. The air was filmed with smoke, fetid enough to have us breathing through our mouths.

Stepping carefully over a puddle of someone's recycled dinner, I surveyed the room. It was small, with no furniture other than a few folding chairs and the table. The adjoining kitchen area was little more than a galley with a rusty sink and a narrow, greasy stove. The tiny counter held an old, triple beam drug scale, and a quantity of plastic bags sized for quick street sales. Probably a little narcotics sideline the three goons dabbled in to while away the time between weapons deliveries.

There were no other rooms or closets, no visible cases of weapons. And no Mr. BIG, unless he was a dwarf who'd chosen to hide in the greasy oven. I could hear my partner talking to the men, inquiring about his gun purchase.

One of the men gestured expansively toward the table.

"Ya wanna smoke, mon? Some blow? It's de finest.

Or some a dis wine?" Breathing heavily, he settled his considerable girth into a folding chair. The butt of a gun protruded from his waistband, nearly eclipsed by his belly. Leering, he waggled his tongue at me.

"C'mon over here, Sweet Thing. I'll get you loosened up, help you relax."

I glanced at my partner. In our years of working together, we'd perfected the art of silent communication. One glance was all it took to tell him the deal was queered. His eyes flashed, briefly, but he smiled at the looming men.

"Business before pleasure, my man. Why don't we take care of my deal first?" There was nothing to do now but play the role and wait for back-up. Leaning back in his chair, Phil glanced around the room. "And where's the man, Bro'? I thought you said he'd be here."

"You got de money, mon?" Melvin paused over his second line of coke. "I'll take de money right now."

A sticky situation, considering Phil had no money. But they didn't have the weapons, so either way, we'd have to do some fancy dancing. At least fifteen minutes worth.

"You'll get the money when I get my shipment," Phil bluffed. "And when I meet the man."

One of the other men belched, tossed his empty wine bottle on the floor. "It ain't like you got a choice, mon," he told Phil. "You give us the money, you give us the bitch. And you get the hell out." Like a black behemoth, he rose and lumbered over to the mattress in the corner. "You don't wanna play by our rules, you lose." Smiling madly, he leaned over to flick aside the mattress. More roaches scattered, and a few mice that had been feasting on the body that lay beneath it. The body of a man who had been dead for days, now gray and gutted like a rotting fish. The black hole at center mass meant a shotgun blast at close range—a swift end for a dissatisfied customer.

Melvin was standing now, absently toying with a stiletto that protruded from his meaty paw. The other two men had gun bores trained on my partner.

"We can all be friends," one of them crooned. "Just give us de money. Den we can all party wit' de girl."

I wish I could tell you that's when our back-up came crashing in, and the good guys prevailed. That would've been the perfect Hollywood ending. But that's not the way it happened. When the first shots spat out from the Jamaican's gun, Phil dived for cover in a room where there was none. Rolling on the filthy floor, he grabbed for the mattress while I kicked over the drug table. It was a diversionary tactic none of them expected. I was the whore, the brainless bimbo provided solely for their pleasure. Grabbing for the gun in my boot, I hoped desperately that the pleasure would be mine.

The table struck the first man, and threw up a screen of flying drugs that obscured visibility in the hazy room. More gun blasts, the rising smell of smoke and cordite, and finally, blood. By the time our back-up team kicked down the door, three people were shot, two were dead. One of them was my partner.

There are no words to describe the moments that followed, nothing that could begin to describe the horror. Even the sight of Melvin, slumped against the wall and drooling blood from the .45 caliber hole in his forehead, did little to assuage the pain. Two squadrols were summoned, one for prisoner transport, the other to carry the dead.

I stayed with Phil as his blood pumped through that ridiculous pimp's suit, held him long after he was gone. And swore that I'd had enough, that I was throwing in the towel that very night. They could have my badge and all the heartbreak that went with it. I wasn't aware that I'd been shot, that my blood mixed with Phil's in those final moments. I'd been lucky. It was a channel wound, a light skimming crease along the skin of my thigh. Not enough to kill me, but enough to leave a scar, and the memory.

I don't remember who took me away, only the rush of other gang officers who converged on the scene. They covered my partner and carried me down the stairs, but outside, I struggled away from them, demanded to stand and wait until Phil was taken away. An ambulance pulled up, next to the squad car that held the two handcuffed goons. As the paramedics helped me inside, one of the goons said, "That's some kinda bitch! Even 'tho she five-0. I still like to get me a piece of that!"

"Then take a good look at that ass," the cop advised before slamming the door. "Cuz that's as close to it as you'll ever get!"

In the movies, the good guys live to fight another day. In real life, one of them was delivered to the morgue. In the movies, the bad guys get what's coming to them. In this particular incident, they got the kind of slick, fast-talking lawyer that mountains of drug money can buy, and greased the wheels of justice. The two surviving goons went to trial, claiming entrapment and evidence tampering. A year later, they were back on the street.

And every time I look at the white-ridged scar on my leg, I think of Phil, and the pain, and the job I vowed to quit years ago. And then I go to work and do it all over again, because I'm a cop. That's what we do.

Youngblood

In street terms, she was a youngblood. Fresh meat to peddle on Clark Street, a gritty strip of winos, junkies and whores who trade flesh for money, money for drugs, drugs for flesh. A continuous loop of sin that keeps the cars trolling and the whores moving from trick to trick.

Even at her tender age—just 14, we found out later—she knew the street's cardinal rule: time is money. A lesson learned from her pimp's fists each time business was slow or her money short. Maurice expected her to be a big earner. He kept her fueled on drugs and fear, taught her how to work the street. Since he'd invested his time, it was up to her to bring in the cash. Such a fine-looking bitch had no excuses. Men liked the young girls—sweet and fresh, no visible scars, no needle marks. Youngblood was all of that.

So she worked the stroll, learned to work fast and keep moving. It was what Maurice wanted. He took care of her out here. Kept the other pimps away, watched out for her while she worked. And rewarded her, at the end of a long night, with enough white powder to bring black oblivion. Nothing that would leave scars. Nothing to mark the merchandise.

They said she was out here for five or six months. Teetering on platform heels, she minced along, strutting narrow hips and coltish legs. The thick make-up she troweled on never quite masked eyes glazed with fatigue and amphetamines, but it didn't matter. Nobody ever looked at her eyes, or much else besides the skimpy spandex shorts and sequined bra. Maurice made sure she dressed to impress.

The other whores watched her. Those who'd been out here long enough, the ones who bore the marks of "the life," had seen girls like her before. She was young and pretty, they said, but not exactly street smart. The young ones like her forget it's just a business and fall in love, usually with the man pouring lies in their ear and dope in their veins. Once that happens, there's trouble. Lovesick whores are the last thing a pimp wants, the first thing he'll get rid of—one way or another. Ways they preferred not to think about.

So they tried to warn her. Tiffany with the orange wig and Pandora of the oozing lesions took Youngblood aside. Tried to school her in the ways a whore has to protect herself, even from her pimp. Didn't pay to be weak when only the strong survive, they said. If she wanted to last, she had to be tough.

Advice that might have been useful had it come earlier. But it was too late—exactly five months late, to be exact. Youngblood was beyond love and moving toward motherhood. She wasn't showing yet, not enough that Maurice would notice. She wanted it to be a surprise. Wanted their baby to be the gift she gave him, the child he'd treasure. Then he'd take her off the street and take care of them all. He said she was beautiful. Their baby would be beautiful too, and their life a dream. With the money he made selling drugs, they could live the high life.

She couldn't decide when to tell him. It had to be special, a tender moment when they were alone. Moments that rarely came now that the weather was warmer. More johns were cruising the stroll, eager for a taste of sin. Maurice made her work longer hours, tougher tricks.

The last guy had pulled a gun. Cocking it, he'd shoved the blue steel muzzle against her head, demanding his pleasure. Youngblood was ready. The other whores had taught her a basic lesson of street survival. Kneeling before him, she slid the razor from her shoe, left him limp and bleeding. It was the first man she'd slashed, the first life she'd taken. Afterward, she bolted down the dark alley, sobbing fitfully.

She couldn't do this anymore, not like that.

Pandora and Tiffany were right. She had to protect herself and this new life inside her. Trembling in the shadows, she waited for her nerves to steady, and her thoughts to clear. It must be instinct she was feeling. She was a mother now, or almost, and had to protect her baby. Maurice's baby. She was going to tell him tonight.

It was Saturday, a big-money night on Clark Street. Cars inched along the drag, men with enough money to fall in lust. On nights like this, Youngblood could make a bundle. Maurice was counting on it. And more than a little annoyed when she had other ideas. She didn't want to work, she told him. It was too dangerous.

"Not as dangerous as my fists," he said, backhanding her quickly. As far as he was concerned, the conversation was over. Usually, one or two slaps was enough, but tonight was different. Sobbing through swollen lips, she shrank back against the wall, away from his swinging fists. *He was going to hurt the baby. She had to protect it.*

Youngblood went limp, a sign Maurice took for compliance. He glared at the weeping girl. Hadn't meant to bruise the merchandise, but sometimes it couldn't be helped. Girls this young required motivation.

He dipped into his pocket, brought out the tiny bag. Maybe a little taste would get her moving.

220

Jerking her head back, he brought the powder up to her nose.

"Snort this," he ordered. "Make you feel better. Then get your ass out on that street."

Youngblood stared at him, wondering which was stronger—fear or instinct?

"No," she said.

Responding to a call of "suspicious persons in the alley," we find their two bodies slumped together like broken puppets. The man's eyes stare vacantly above the gaping hole, a slashed neck courtesy of the razor still clutched in the young girl's fist. She's pitched forward at an odd angle, curled beneath the booted foot he used to stomp her. Fluids still seep from their lifeless bodies: his, hers, and the fetus that's pulped on the bloody cinders.

Swan Song

Cancer, they'd said. Too far gone, by the time it was detected, for treatment to do any good. There were medications, of course, to make him more comfortable. Things that could make what time he had left as painless as possible. But nothing that would take away the feelings, like the outrage that made him want to punch holes in the walls, choke the somber, blank-faced doctors who delivered the news. Or the despair that kept his guts roiling when he considered what they'd given him. A death sentence at twenty-six? What kind of benevolent God allowed such a thing?

There were so many things he wanted to do, places he'd dreamed of visiting. Dreams that were shattered with a single word, replaced by a chilling image of hospital rooms, bleeping machines, tubes and wires attached to his wasting body. His kind of cancer wasn't negotiable, they'd said. No matter how many deals he made with God, the outcome would be the same.

It wasn't the way Frank Sebastian intended to die. A sterile room attended by sympathetic strangers who tracked his dying by grams and milliliters was not the end he'd pictured, not at this age or any other. He didn't want sympathy, and he sure as hell didn't want an audience while he slipped away, fighting a battle he'd never win.

His hand cradled the grips of the blue steel .38, clicked the loaded cylinder into place. It was better this way. A last-ditch effort at zero hour to control his own destiny, orchestrate his end the way he thought it should be. Fear had his hands trembling and his stomach knotted. Did he have the guts to pull this off? Probably what everyone wondered the first time they fired a gun. In his case, the last time. There was no way out now, no other choices. Just raise the damn gun and get it over with.

Waiting outside in the idling Ford, LeeAnne O'Shea watched the liquor store's door. Since the store windows were covered with posters and signs, she couldn't see the interior, had no idea if Frankie was okay. Three minutes, max, he'd said. Just run in, get the money and hit the highway. In a couple days they'd be sipping Margaritas on a Mexican beach.

A blast of gun shots followed by the crash of breaking glass had her cringing.

Five shots or six? Frankie's gun or...? But here he came, dashing through the door, weaving crazily toward the car.

"Just *drive!*" he shouted as he dived inside. "Get

me the fuck out of here!"

They sped two miles west down Wilson Avenue before she dared to breathe. By that time he'd yanked off the ski mask, brushed off the glass chips that clung to his clothes. He showed her the bulging paper bag, upending it ceremoniously on the seat between them. A shower of currency fluttered down—tens, twenties, fifties, more than she'd imagined.

"Jesus, Frankie! I never figured you'd get so much!"

"We hit 'em at a good time. They were getting their receipts ready to take to the bank. And there's more." He dug into the pockets of his camouflage jacket.

A bottle of Tequila came next, and several spools of Instant Lottery tickets.

"Pin money," he grinned. "For the trip to the border. I bet there's a few grand here, just from the tickets alone." Already he could visualize the miles of sparkling beaches, the breezy tropical nights. To hell with cancer and hospitals and the grim business of dying. There'd be sun and surf and the woman he loved, not the worst way for a man to go out. He cracked open the tequila bottle and took a hearty swig.

LeeAnne executed a neat turn onto Western Avenue. The traffic was heavier here, slowed by lumbering trucks and road construction. Inching along behind a delivery truck, they were hemmed in by a station wagon on one side, a pick-up on the other.

"This ain't smart, LeeAnne. Get off this damn street and cut over to the expressway. We gotta make tracks."

"I'm *tryin'*, Frankie."

It was another mile before the last of the construction barriers. Finally the road opened up and LeeAnne could accelerate.

"See? We'll make some good time now. Soon as I can turn off..." Reaching over, she gave his arm a squeeze, yelping when her fingers sank into wet red.

"Oh, my God! Is that—"

"It's nothing. Just a nick from the glass." Chugging more tequila, he pointed to the right. "There's room there in front of that Mazda. Cut over and you can hang a turn. Get us the hell off this street."

"But you're *bleeding*, Frankie!" LeeAnne leaned over, reaching under the seat. "There's a first aid kit here. You better—"

Shrieking airbrakes pulled her attention back to the road. The truck in front of them had slammed to a stop, too fast and too close for LeeAnne to react. The truck's steel tailgate loomed ahead like a mouth about to swallow them whole.

That evening, the accident got extensive coverage on all four of the local news channels. Reported as one of the worst accidents in recent Chicago history, news anchors showed on-scene film clips of the grisly wreckage. It was a domino effect, they said, initiated by a driver who swerved to avoid a dog. The resultant pile-up included three trucks, eight cars, and a total of twenty-one people killed. Victims' identities had yet to be released, pending notification of their families.

What the news reports failed to mention was that the crush of twisted steel was so severe, rescue teams called to the scene used torches to extricate some of the bodies. And that one of the three survivors, Frank Sebastian, had been pinned beneath the Ford's dashboard, unable to move as he watched his girl-friend slowly die. Blood-soaked money and strips of lottery tickets still clung to his body when they finally lifted him out. Hot tears tracked his face when he heard a gaping cop say, "I don't fuckin' believe *this...*"

Perfect

I thought it was perfect. To a kid just barely twenty-three, it seemed like the world. What could be better than being a cop? Cops were the good guys who saved the day, found the lost kids, allowed citizens to rest easy at night knowing they were protected. Cops caught the bad guys. Cops got respect.

I remember that first day at the Police Academy. Three hundred new recruits sat in the gym bleachers, some scared, some nervous, all trying to look as tough as the old vets on hand to give us the Department welcome. Speeches that were meant as a welcome, but only served to scare us more. I can still remember parts of them.

The scowling Captain Benedict, former Marine and self-described ass-kicker, got straight to the point.

"One thing you all need to realize now, and for the rest of the time you're on this job, is that you are the MAN. Once you put on that uniform, you are a target. People will call you for help, but they'll resent you while you're helping them. Most folks don't like us, a lot of 'em hate us. There's a lot of folks out there who'd like to see us dead and do their damnedest to make that happen. Get used to it. This job ain't no popularity contest. If you want to be a hero, you shoulda joined the Fire Department."

None of us dared to breathe. His speech was scary as hell and twenty times more exciting. Sure, we knew the job was dangerous, but that was part of the thrill. To a young guy like me it was also a sense of belonging and the glamour that came with the uniform. The badge and the gun were the symbols of our office: protectors and peacekeepers. The Man.

I remember looking around at the assembled recruits—strangers who'd become my brothers in arms. For the first time, I felt that I belonged. Those nameless faces were my new family who would back me up, go with me daily into the fray, maybe one day save my ass or I theirs. We were brothers together, a protective circle. At the time, I believed it.

Is there any greater sense of accomplishment than the first time you strap on the gun belt and pin on your badge? The stranger in the mirror, trim in regulation blues and Sam Brown leather, stares back impassively, just a bit menacing. There's a gun at your hip and flint in your eyes and that comical square-jawed resolve most rookies strive for. I was determined to fight the world's wrongs—and win. I was ready to take on the bad guys, kick ass, take names—a public servant on a mission. I was going to do it all.

Those first days on the street, I learned about another job perk: the women who love a man in uniform. I was young and eager to have my share. Could it possibly get any better than this? A virtual smorgasbord of women drawn to the danger of a cop's life. The cop-fuck fantasies fueled by their imagination and a steady diet of TV cop shows.

I know now it's all part of the hype assigned to law-enforcers by a curious public. We're the modern day cowboys, the last of the gunslingers. In lieu of shoot-outs at O.K. Corral, we handle the drive-bys, the burglars, the knife-wielding rapists. And if, in the process, we catch a bullet in the leg, maybe get slashed in the back, it doesn't matter. We're the tough guys, the first string sent in where angels fear to tread. Injuries are part of the gig, more fodder for our war stories, more scars to display to some wide-eyed cop groupie who hangs on every word. We piss vinegar and spit blood and never stop doing what cops do. Serve and protect, that's our gig. At the time, I believed it all.

It's hard to say exactly when reality struck. There was no single incident that was my wake-up call. When you work the streets, it doesn't happen like that. Like puberty, it's a gradual process that takes time to develop—thoughts and feelings that simmer for months or years before it reaches the boiling point. You feel the twinges of something different, feelings that weren't there before, until the day you wake up with a raging erection and think, "Goddamn! Where did THAT come from?"

A street cop's life is like that—feelings that shift and fester and finally become a major hard-on. And it all starts with the best intentions. You think that you're helping. Eventually, you realize there's no helping some people, that they're determined to go to hell on a bobsled and take you with them.

Take, for example, the countless domestic disturbances you're called on to referee. Domestics take up roughly 60% of a street cop's work assignment. Someone's always kicking ass, or getting theirs kicked in the name of love and domestic bliss. When the police arrive, he's drunk, she's bloody and screaming revenge. Shouting that she wants his worthless ass locked up, she's through with him, time for a divorce. You couldn't agree more. Her nose is still oozing blood and her eyes are pulped like jelly. Any bastard who does that to his wife deserves to get locked up. But as soon as you snap on the handcuffs, her story changes.

Suddenly *you're* the bad guy, the oppressive bastard who's taking her man away. And suddenly this poor, battered, bloody woman is punching and biting, kicking and shrieking, but it's you that's the target this time. You're the Man. And even though this scene replays *ad nauseum* throughout your career, you still don't understand. In a perfect world, people would try to get along. But who's to say what's perfect?

I thought I had it figured out once. Had a mental list of all life's perfect moments—the ones I felt were indisputable. Like the moment you hold your new baby in your arms, feel the surge of love so strong you can barely contain it. It's a miracle. This new life you've helped create is now cradled in your arms.

Stroking that velvety baby skin, you wonder if anything can be sweeter. But the job teaches you that, for some people, the answer is obviously yes. Like those who toss their newborns in a dumpster just minutes after birth. It happens all the time. And when the 911 call comes, it's the police who are sent to the scene, who fish out the tiny body from the pile of reeking trash. A job for the MAN—to hold the corpse of a child whose birth and death were just minutes apart, thanks to an unloving parent. Part of the job, cleaning up an imperfect world's dirty deeds. You remind yourself that these same baby-killers are part of the community you protect, for whom you swore to lay down your life. Now you're not sure which of you is crazier.

Eventually, I learned that sanctuary was necessary to keep me sane—some warm place where I could retreat. I thought it was my marriage. The street was the raging whore that sucked me dry; my wife the lady who replenished me. She was patient, sweet, a soothing balm for the oozing wounds that never healed. Wounds on my heart and soul she couldn't see, couldn't begin to imagine.

She thought I was strong. Brave to do my job each day, stare down the demons. But what she took for strength was an enforced detachment so I wouldn't feel, wouldn't have to acknowledge fear or pain or any emotion that interfered with my duty. How else could I gun down a killer—just an eleven year old boy high on drugs and booze and a street gang's attentions? They'd placed the gun in his hand, I put the bullet in his heart. I didn't feel brave then. Easier to face a gunman than his mother's eyes. The look in them and the words she sobbed have never left me: "You say he was a gang member? He was a lonely little boy. You are in a gang, too, no? And today, your gang wins."

So I numbed myself, a thick professional callous that allowed me to function, kept me intact. Hardened myself to the pain and the questions with no answers. The ones I never dreamed about when life was perfect.

There is no lasting sanctuary—another reality of a cop's life. My marriage faded. I was hard, she said. Unfeeling. So remote, I was like a stranger, and we never seemed to talk anymore.

What was there to talk about? How I saw my

children's faces in every kid on the street? That my nightmares featured my family, brutalized by the vicious thugs I encountered nightly? Dreams in which I couldn't help them, was too late to save them. Just as it happened in life to all the victims I couldn't help, the corpses who stared in silent reproach. I had no words for that, or most of what my life had become. She wasn't out there, she'd never understand. She wasn't part of that circle of my life, that one that grew increasingly smaller.

Cops live insular lives. It's an us-against-them mentality that begins in the Academy and grows rampant. We're the infantry on the front lines. Everyone else is the audience, watching our lives on the evening news. Another burglary, robbery, homicide? We're there. Our job is a contact sport with victories and defeats non-players can't understand unless they've been on the field. Most people wouldn't want to be.

The divorce made me philosophical. It was part of dues, more fallout from the job. Worse than any whore, it demanded every ounce of my commitment, every minute of my time. Invaded my dreams even in my off-time, influencing the way I lived, the way I thought, the friends I kept. Friends? Only cops inhabited my social circle—the only ones who understood. Their seasoned eyes reflect the same scenes, the same dead visions. Co-survivors of the same war. Among them, I didn't have to detach. I didn't have to be anybody. By that time, I didn't know who I was.

Funny how the years slip by. Strange that I don't recall them passing, but can still summon particular images with laser clarity. All of them from this job that I thought was perfect. The helpless kids, the sick and old, the parade of bodies savaged beyond recognition. All of it grisly baggage that cops carry, street-issued scenes that never fade.

I've seen it all. Thought, at the beginning, that I knew it all, knew exactly what I was meant to do, and how I'd do it. The perfect blueprint for my life. Looking at it from this end, things are much different. I realize now there's only one thing I know, and that's how to make a perfect exit.

She's here beside me, my faithful friend who's been with me to hell and back. My .357 magnum, the service revolver I bought back at the beginning. A vicious bitch when necessary, she's sleek blue steel, a spitfire with a lethal kiss. The only kiss I want now, the one that will send me to sweet slumber and lay my nightmares to rest.

Everything is ready. When you read this note, whoever you are, I know you'll understand. In lieu of dreams realized, there's only the foolish illusions of the naive. I played the game, I accept defeat, and now, with this single bullet, I'll cut my losses. The perfect ending to an imperfect life. I pray for grace under this last pressure. Load the bullet, click the cylinder into place, pucker up for the spitfire's kiss...and wait for peace...

A misfire! Last damn bullet I have and it didn't work! I can't believe it. Can't even make a graceful exit. The story of my life: nothing is perfect.

www.bluemurder.com